LIVING ART

Published in 2020 by Areca Books Asia Sdn Bhd
70 Lebuh Acheh, 10200 Penang, Malaysia
www.arecabooks.com

Text © Emelia Ong
Photographs © DL Studios
Edited by Joanne Lai
Design and layout by Malvina Anthony
Printed by Phoenix Press Sdn Bhd, Malaysia

Cover photo: Prints produced by 'Buku Jalanan Ranau', a collective initiated in 2016 to promote a reading culture amongst youth in Ranau, through free book loans and reading groups. The prints were produced during a workshop (2017) at the Pangrok Sulap studio-cum-gallery.

Back cover: Group photo of Pangrok Sulap, courtesy of Julia Chan.

Perpustakaan Negara Malaysia   Cataloguing-in-Publication Data

Ong, Emelia
    Living Art: The inspired lives of 14 Malaysian artists & their art practice / Emelia Ong.
    ISBN 978-967-5719-40-0
    1. Art – Malaysia.
    2. Artists – Malaysia – Anecdotes.
    3. Art, Malaysian
    I. Title.
    709.9595

Areca Books is a niche publisher based in Penang, Malaysia. The imprint has a proud reputation for producing richly illustrated publications that celebrate *genius loci* and a sense of place in multicultural Malaysia. Its pioneering works are enduring contributions to the fields of cultural heritage, social history, visual arts, architecture and the environment of Southeast Asia.

LIVING ART

The inspired lives of 14 Malaysian artists & their art practice

EMELIA ONG

 ARECA BOOKS

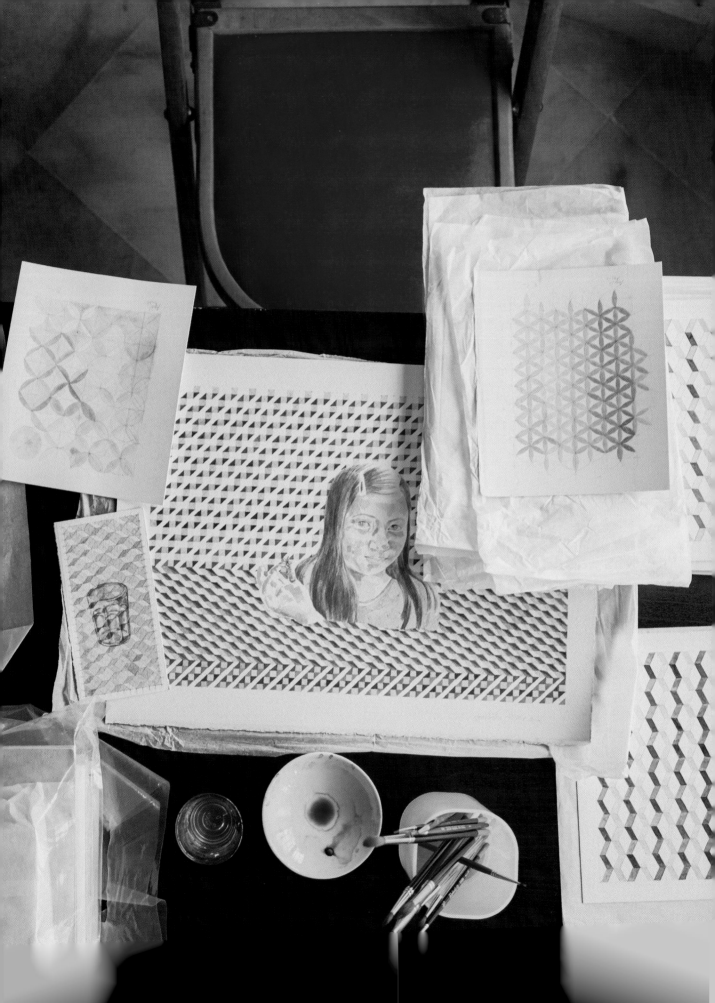

CONTENTS

7
Foreword

9
Introduction

11
MAD ANUAR ISMAIL
The Art of Craft

21
NOOR MAHNUN
MOHAMED
The Relentless Pursuit of
Enduring Beauty

29
SHARON CHIN
Transformative Spaces

39
ABDUL MANSOOR
IBRAHIM
Quiet Impressions

47
HASNUL J SAIDON
Entangled Bodies of Energy

57
GAN CHIN LEE
The Art of Balance

65
JENNIFER LIU HSIN YING
Liberated Bodies

73
ISE
The Indefinable Art of Being

83
ELIAS YAMANI
Everyday Objects, Alternate
Worlds

91
EIFFEL CHONG
Uncovering Life's Disguises

99
AZZAHA IBRAHIM
Building Upon Our Artistic
Pasts

107
SHIA YIH YIING
The Art of Innocence and
Experience

115
ILSE NOOR
Wondrous Landscapes:
Histories, Legends and Myths

125
PANGROK SULAP
Grassroots Ethos of Punk

136
Acknowledgements

FOREWORD

BY DOLORES WHARTON

"Dear Dolores," Emelia wrote, "I am in the midst of completing my coffee-table book and was hoping you would write the foreword. I think it is appropriate since you were the one who published the first interviews on the contemporary Malaysian artists."

I was exhilarated by the honor! It was in 1971 that my book, *Contemporary Artists of Malaysia: A Biographic Survey*, had been published. Furthermore, to be remembered after all these years was an enormous compliment. Also, Emelia's method as scribe echoes my own and brilliantly illuminates the current Malaysian art scene.

Her book, *Living Art*, is an exuberant celebration of the activism at play in the Malaysian culture today. Her explorations into the works and humanity of 14 leading artists serve as stages to illuminate each artist's influence, medium and material preferences. Through their responses and informal expositions given in interviews, we learn of the new developments and directions under way, as these creative people take their places in the dynamic local art scene. Key to the success and joy of the book is Emelia's presentation of the artwork, a treasure trove of handsomely displayed studies offered to engage our spirit and our senses.

Although Emelia has written her book for the lay audience, a more worldly literati will equally enjoy and appreciate her scholarship as an art historian. I, having had the extraordinary good fortune to become acquainted with a large portion of the Malayan and later Malaysian region some 50 years ago, am overjoyed to learn further about its richness as presented in *Living Art*.

It is a great honor for me to have been asked to play a role in this celebration as a dedicated friend and ardent admirer.

Dolores Wharton is a civic leader and arts advocate. She founded the Fund for Corporate Initiatives, and served on the board of directors of many institutions including the Museum of Modern Art in New York and the National Council on the Arts in America. She resided in Southeast Asia from 1958 to 1964 and is the author of *Contemporary Artists of Malaysia: A Biographic Survey* (1971).

NOTE TO READERS

This book seeks to present art through its practice. It approaches art, not only through artworks but through the processes involved in the making of art, as told in the voices of the artists themselves. Through a series of interviews, 14 artists share their personal stories and divulge intimate insights on why art is an inspiring and fundamental endeavour intrinsic to them.

The artists featured represents the diversity of art practice in Malaysia today. They demonstrate an inclusive variety of art forms, encompassing drawings, paintings, sculpture, printmaking, assemblage, installation, performance art, photography and multimedia.

These candid interviews also offer a demystifying view of the artists, enabling a more approachable and expanded view of the artist as researcher/curator/ designer/illustrator/educator/ activist.

Each interview addresses six main aspects of how art intersects the lives of the artists:

1. **Growing Up**: What childhood experiences/influences inspired their first forays into the artistic medium of expression?

2. **Learning Process**: What were the significant milestones in their journey that shaped the way they practiced art today?

3. **Space and Place**: How is the location and set-up of the studio important and influential to the types of works produced?

4. **Current Practice**: How do they approach their current practice, in terms of genre, subject matter and content?

5. **Working Process**: What is the structure of a typical work-day for them, and what specific process keeps them motivated?

6. **Materials and Tools**: How they engage with their materials; do they master/adapt/ modify or breakaway from traditional usage of tools/materials/techniques?

An introductory essay precedes each interview, to situate their practice within general art historical contexts. It highlights why certain spaces, styles, medium, techniques or approaches are privileged above others in their individual approaches, with insight on their unique personal histories.

It also explains how these individual approaches towards work have helped them resolve or challenge certain conventions in artistic practice, and how each of them continue to derive meaning in their lives through the process of art making.

ACKNOWLEDGEMENTS

To all the featured artists, I truly appreciate our conversations and time spent together. Many thanks to David Lok and his brilliant crew of photographers at DL Studios: Sok Lin, Xin Lee, Kecik Sin and Ikram Yusof. My sincere thanks also to: Salmmyah Raheem, my GRA, for the transcribing of interviews and translation work; Ngan Chew Pei for interviews in Mandarin; Sooshie Sulaiman, John Lim of The Edge Galerie, and Assoc. Prof. Dr. Mohd. Nasir Hashim, Director of the Cultural Center at UM. I would also like to take this chance to remember those who have inspired me through their enduring commitments in their own fields; be it editing, writing, researching, collecting, curating, making, or teaching art; this includes, the late Redza Piyadasa, Izmer Ahmad, T. K. Sabapathy, Beverly Yong, Zain Azahari, Pakhruddin Sulaiman, Clare Tan, Kelvin Chuah, Simon Soon, Yau Bee Ling and Siaw Mei Li. Last but not least, to my parents, my dear husband Roshan, my kids, Yoshua and Yohanna, and my parents-in-law, for all their love. This book project is funded by the University of Malaya BKP grant.

ABOUT THE AUTHOR

Emelia Ong Ian Li is currently a Senior Lecturer, teaching Malaysian Art History in the Visual Arts MA programme at the Cultural Centre in the University of Malaya (UM). A specialist in the Visual Arts field, Emelia received her BFA in Graphic Design from the University of Bridgeport in Connecticut, USA, and earned her MA in Visual Arts at the University of Malaya under the supervision of renowned Malaysian pioneer art historian, the late Redza Piyadasa. She then completed her PhD at Universiti Sains Malaysia (USM), Penang, with a thesis on the construction of identities through art practice during the independence period of Malaysia. Emelia's research interests include modern and contemporary Malaysian and Southeast Asian art, and its intersections with culture, identity, tradition and nationalism. Currently, she is researching local art practices as processes of personal and social meaning-making.

ABOUT THE EDITOR

Joanne Lai Chia Yin currently teaches Design Reflective Practice at Universiti Tunku Abdul Rahman (UTAR). During her PhD candidacy with the Sainsbury Research Unit for the Arts of Africa, Oceania & the Americas (SRU) UK, she embarked on extensive ethnographic research immersed with the indigenous Kadazan-Dusun communities in Sabah, while exploring their contemporary practice of ritual, festival, art and cultural identity. Enjoying a breadth of influence from an interdisciplinary academic perspective, her research interests also include Anthropology, Museology, Pre-modern Southeast Asian Art History and the Natural Sciences.

MAD ANUAR
THE ART OF CRAFT

Mad Anuar is a sculptor who works primarily with wood and metal, creating large-scale, three-dimensional artworks inspired by Malay folklore and traditional motifs, as well as aspects of everyday life at sea. His subject matter includes stylized figurative compositions, often featuring the *keris*[1] and the boat as prominent recurring motifs, amongst other traditional Malay iconography. He spent his childhood in Kuala Terengganu and was immersed at a young age, in the craft life of the village where his artisan neighbours were skilled in traditional forms of boat building, house building, wood carving and forging the *keris*. He graduated from Institut Teknologi MARA (ITM)[2] in 1977 and continues to pursue his lifelong passion in creating Malay traditional art through the medium of contemporary sculpture.

Mad recalls that by the time he began his studies at ITM, he had already amassed a working knowledge of traditional wood carving as a boat designer in Terengganu. Thus, he was not easily impressed with Western forms of building and art making. What interested him as a student of art, however, were the western aesthetic concepts which separated Art from the works of Craft. His encounter with Western modernist sculptures allowed him the liberty to experiment with more ambitious forms and aesthetics, which were completely unrelated to the functionality of boat building and decorative carving traditions. He became

inspired to create works of art that were made purely for the pleasure inherent in their making.

He asserts that his approach towards sculpture must be differentiated from those of the Western vitalist sculptors, for although they do emphasize the metaphysical aspects of materials, their emphasis is located squarely within the remit of the artist to enable its manifestation. In contrast, when Mad Anuar approaches a piece of wood, he acknowledges the spirit inherent in the wood and allows this to affect the final outcome of the artwork. Every piece is a negotiation between the will of the wood and the will of the artist. The final sculpture is thus the embodiment of this unity of spirits – that of the material and the artist. Unlike many a Western contemporary artist who avoids talking about craftsmanship for fear of being labelled a mere craftsman, Mad has no qualms with that label, and jokingly acknowledges that he is from the 'old school'.

Upon graduation, he began producing larger sculptures. As casting is a costly technique in terms of material and space, he needed an alternative method which did not require the use of heavy industrial machinery. By experimenting with using flat bars that are welded together to form a skin-like covering for the underlying framework, Mad Anuar developed a unique welding method for the production of his metal works. His staple equipment comprises no

The Studio Pena art collective members meet around this simple table daily to chat, eat, and create art. From left to right: Mad Anuar, Madzi@Fuad Pathil, a visitor, Mansoor Ibrahim.

more than five different types of chisels and the basic tools typically found in any carpenter's toolbox: wrenches, pliers, shears, hammers, torches, hacksaws, goggles and gloves. Similarly, his process of transposing a small two-dimensional sketch to a three-dimensional larger-than-life sculpture, though deceptively simple, is nonetheless a feat of masterful craftsmanship. He creates sketches which consist of just a few lines indicating the general form of the design, rather than delineating it according to accurate measurements as some sculptors would do. Once this quick sketch is done, he starts to work instinctively and is driven by the intuitive handling of the materials.

Today, Mad Anuar shares a collective space with a few other artists at Studio Pena in Kuala Lumpur. This open studio is housed behind the writers' collective, Rumah Pena.[3] In 1998, Mad Anuar started working in the open space behind Rumah Pena with the late Sutung Umar RS,[4] at the invitation of Baharuddin Zainal a.k.a. Baha Zain, who was then the deputy director of Rumah Pena. The group later expanded with the inclusion of ceramicists Fauzi Tahir, printmaker Mansoor Ibrahim and American sculptor Helen Betlem. Together, they formed

the pioneer artists of Studio Pena, which held art workshops and opened its doors to international art students during its heyday.

GROWING UP

Can you remember your first exposure to art?

When I was little, I lived in Kuala Terengganu. I used to go 'disturb' the traditional boat and house builders who were master artisans in my village. There were many such workshops. So, I just snooped around and whenever they threw away any wood, I would pick it up and try to work with it. My hands would bleed because I didn't know how to use a *parang* (traditional machete). Then they told me, 'Not like that, hold it like this.' That's how I learned. They made big boats, I made small ones.

I particularly remember an incident with a beautiful and strong *langsat*[5] tree. I thought it was a good size to work with, so I cut it down. Oh! They were so mad at me! They said, 'Do you know how long it took for it to grow that big?' I was just a child, how could I have known? I was about six years old. I used to watch them while they made their *keris* (traditional Malay dagger), so I wanted to make one myself.

You could use a parang at six years of age?

No! [laughs] But I did it anyway. I loved it. I would just wrap my hands up and get on with it.

Finally, when I was 20 years old, I became an apprentice. That's when I learnt the correct methods of carving and boat building, and I became a boat designer.

When I enrolled at ITM, I was already 23 years old. All the other kids were about 18 years old.

LEARNING PROCESS

When I first started, I asked myself, 'What should my first step be?' There were not many books available on traditional Malay aesthetics or Malay philosophy. Then I realized that the knowledge I needed would not be contained in just one book but, rather, embodied in literature, folk stories, sayings, poems. So, I studied traditional art and woodcarving which were often inspired by those sources. For that purpose, I travelled to Kedah, Johor, Kelantan and Terengganu in order to interview the *datuk purba* (ancient masters) of Kelantan, such as the renowned *wayang kulit* (shadow puppetry) expert Pak Nik Man bin Pak Dir, who was then advisor to the National Museum.

How long did you do that for?

For about nine years. During that time, I was working as a designer for the government, and the head of the workshop then was Tengku Ibrahim.[6] He was the old master, father of Tengku Sabri. So, for eight years I studied under his expertise. Before that I worked with Wan Su.[7] That's when I learnt the finer details of Malay woodcarving.

I remember asking Tengku Ibrahim, 'How do I learn about the trees? And the flowers?' He told me, 'That's easy… go sleep with them!' So I did. I started sleeping at the plant nursery! After that, I understood. Not straightaway, no; but eventually, I understood.

There are vibrations, you see? If you sit still and stay with the trees, you will feel it after a long while. There are no words to describe this. Some say it's intuition. But you start to look at the tree, and then you realise, 'Eh… I know you.'

SPACE AND PLACE

I have a studio at home. I used to have one in Ulu Kelang before moving it to my house. Later, upon the invitation of the director at Pena, Dato' Baha Zain and the secretary, I moved my workspace to Studio Pena.

In 1992 or 1993, I was still working from home. At that time, my kids were still in secondary school and I would fetch them to and from school. Once they had all gone off to university, I moved here to Studio Pena in 2002.

In 2002, Akademi Pena had just been shut down, and Studio Pena was born. At first we were not stationed here exactly [at the present location] but we were located in the field near the carpark. Fauzi [a pioneer member of Studio Pena] set up two big umbrellas in the field and we worked under that! Whenever it started to thunderstorm, we ran for shelter. That was how we worked [laughs].

'Storm Rider No. 17'. C2014. Mad's Storm Rider series of sculptures embody the spirit of those who work at sea and brave the storms every single day.

FAUZI TAHIR

Is it important for you to be close to nature?

I used to live by the sea. I feel like I am a part of the natural environment. I think that's important to me. If I am dislocated from that environment for too long, like, if I lived near the supermarkets or behind enclosed walls, I grow weary. It gets too much, after a while.

What is your ideal space?

Ah... at first, it was comfortable here. There was enough space to work with, enough space for the tools. But after a while, the things kept adding up. Aiyoh! There was no more space to move around in. No space for displays. Completed works were sitting together with raw materials. No proper storage areas. When you work with wood, you need large storage areas because the seasoning process takes time. We may cut down a piece of wood today only to use it in ten years time.

Have you ever worked in a residency?

I can't. They say, 'Okay you can work here, but you have to be clean.' I say, 'Thank you very much, but I'm not interested.' I can't work under those conditions; I have all kinds of stuff.

CURRENT PRACTICE

Tell us about the type of works you did when you first started working here.

It all actually started with a particular tree that was being chopped down by DBKL,[8] opposite the road from Rumah Pena in 1998. I told Fauzi, 'Can you ask them to throw the wood over here [in front of Rumah Pena]?' It was more convenient for them to put it here than to lug it all the way back home, so they agreed. Then Sutung came along and said, 'What are you all doing? So much wood!' I said, 'Yes, this is good wood. We can use it for sculpture.' So that was the first piece of wood I worked on.

What kind of wood is it?

We call it *Pukul Lima*, in English it is known as Rain Tree.[9] It was very huge, and I have three pieces of sculpture with me, carved from that first piece of wood.

The largest sculpture is entitled *Homage*

to the Mother which embodies the ultimate positive in human nature. It bears the holy inscription of *Bismillahir Rahmanir Rahim* (In the Name of God, the Most Gracious and Most Merciful). Here *Bismillah* is representative of the all-giving Father, and *Rahim* (Womb) is the merciful Mother. Taken together, these words which form the very first sentence at the beginning of the Quran also contain the Father/Mother procreative principle; this embodies the source of the ultimate beginning of humanity, a creative source that is all good.

I also worked on two more pieces. These three pieces (yet to be carved) are the last of that very first *Pukul Lima* tree. Right now, I'm also simultaneously working on stainless steel rod sculptures that are to be hung on walls, and a wood sculpture which is a commissioned piece.

MATERIALS AND TOOLS

Where do you get your materials?

For the metals, I buy them directly from the metal supplier in Sungai Besi. He actually supplies the materials for heavy industries to other countries like China.

I usually buy the five millimeter rods for the frame. For the surface materials, I use a one-inch flat bar which is the easiest to manipulate. When people look at it, they might say that this technique is too time-consuming. But this is how I choose to work because I don't own a foundry. Usually, others will use a plate. With that technique, they would burn and forge and mould. It's all really noisy work. I don't like it. When I work, it's really quiet. I tear it down, I fix it, I weld it and it's finished. I don't even use a grinder. I want the surface texture to be rough, so I leave it in its natural state. Once I am done, I apply the anti-rust. I use car lacquer because it's really durable and there would be no need for polishing after that.

How about your material source for the wood sculptures?

For wood sculptures, I get the materials from the *stor kayu* (wood stores). I don't use commercial woods because they are very expensive. If I buy *cengal*[10] wood commercially, a four-by-four inch beam sells for RM10 per foot. As I need many feet of

Top left: The artist's essential tools. From left to right: wood file, carving knife, rasper, gouge, chisel, nail chisel, saw.

Top right: Stacks of different varieties of seasoned wood such as penaga laut (*Alexandrian Laurel, Calophyllum inophyllum*), ciku (*Sapodilla, Manilkara zapota*), kemuning (*Merrillia, Murraya paniculata*) in his current wood store, collected since 2002.

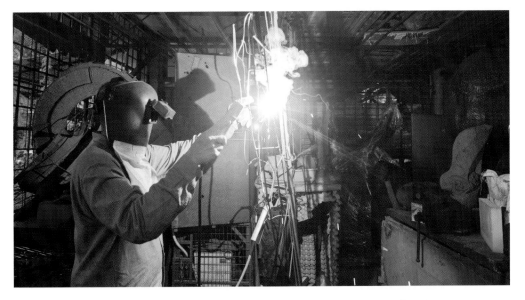

Above: For protection against arc rays and welding sparks, Mad wears a helmet and a long sleeved shirt. In order to dissipate the fumes generated by the welding process, the studio is well-ventilated with open-air grilles on all sides. He uses a TIG (Tungsten Inert Gas) welding machine.

Right: The artist's helmet and gloves sit atop some tools and detritus of metal left over from his previous works.

A quick drawing to capture the design for a wood sculpture inspired by the bird-of-paradise.

timber for my larger works, one piece of wood would cost up to RM180. That's just crazy. Wood in Malaysia is way too expensive, so I don't buy commercial wood for my materials.

Actually, in Malaysia, we have such a huge variety of wood, such as mahogany, acacia, *et cetera*. I also used to 'hijack' these unwanted woods whenever people started cutting trees down. That would be the easiest way. Whenever I see people cutting down trees, I just go over to them and request, '*Bang, tolong buang sini*' ('Brother, please discard the wood over here'). But not every type of wood is suitable for sculpture. For example, Chinese folks like *pokok sena* (angsana),[11] and there are lots of these trees around. But it's extremely difficult to cure the wood, as the *bubuk* (wood-boring beetles)[12] love it.

If we want to cure these *pokok sena*, we need to soak them in running water and wait for the resin to come out. Rubberwood[13] is another type of wood that termites love. In the rubberwood industry, once they chop the trees down, they must immediately throw it into the pond to soak. If this is delayed, the wood may acquire a grey stain. Once that happens, the wood is not *laku* (desirable) anymore.

What kinds of finishing do you use?

There are so many ways to achieve a good finishing. You can use linseed oil or shellac. I use linseed oil to preserve the wood, and then I stain it before I apply the lacquer. I use water-based stains which are fast-drying. You can also use acrylics but the layers must not be applied too thickly. You need to mix it and dilute it well so that it can be absorbed into the wood. But I personally don't use many colours, as I only need shades of brown.

Can you tell us about your essential tools?

My tools are very basic and I have very few items. I don't need them to be sophisticated at all, just as long as I can use them. Unlike my old mentor, the late Tengku Ibrahim… Woah! He had hundreds of chisels! I work with only two or three. This goes for nails as well. If he were to see my tools today, he'd be furious, as I only own a handful [laughs].

WORKING PROCESS

Can you describe your typical working day?

I really don't have a 'standard' day. I usually start around noon and work until about 4 p.m. Most days I don't work past 4 p.m.; I will work seven days a week if I don't have anything else planned during the weekend.

Can you describe your working process?

When I look at a piece of wood I really need to know what kind of forms I can produce from it. There are certain 'restrictions' to be observed when you are working with wood. As it is a 'living material', I cannot 'force' the wood to conform to my will. The form that it will eventually take would have to be already inherent in the core of the wood itself. So I actually have to 'negotiate' with the essence of the wood in order to understand what is actually possible.

This process is intrinsically different from the Western idea of 'process'. When they say 'embodiment', they usually mean that the artist makes the decision to manipulate the form of the wood, fully exercising his will upon the material to imbue a particular rationale onto the form.

The way I approach the term 'embodiment', is with the understanding that there is already an 'embodied' spirit or animus within the material that precedes me. Therefore it would not be appropriate for me to enforce my will upon it. My process is, instead, more of a negotiation with the animus within the wood.

Unfinished work, based on the bird-of-paradise design sketch above. Wood. (Photo courtesy of Fauzi Tahir)

Mad Anuar working on his current project, which consists of stainless steel rods manipulated into three dimensional motifs. To weld the frame, he hangs them on a simple bar that is attached to the ceiling for easy maneuvering. He works on a few different structures like this simultaneously.

So the eventual form is a production of our mutual interaction. This symbiosis is the key to facilitate the final form of the artwork. In this sense, the final artwork is actually a revelation of the essential form that was originally 'embodied' within the wood. This is a similar method used by ancient *keris* craftsmen, when they create the *hulu keris* (keris hilts).

Can you give us an example of this process at work?

When I was working on the *Pukul Lima*, I looked at the wood for a long time. I wanted to proceed with it but was afraid. The kind of character I wanted to portray with the wood was one that was full of lust and greed. An embodiment of disobedience and lust. I kept asking myself, 'How should I proceed?' Finally I did it. I inscribed the Jawi script *Bismillahir Rahmanir Rahim* onto the sculpture. It is not obvious, but if you look closely you will see it. I had transformed it into something good and entitled it 'Homage to the Mother'.

Another smaller sculpture, resulting from this same piece of wood, resembles a pair of downcast human faces. As manifestations of the 'naughty' aspects of human lust and greed, they embody destructive forces which are the opposite of that first sculpture. At the moment, they are still untitled as I consider them still 'works-in-progress'. They have

yet to be resolved into their final form. So for the time being, I see them as 'masks', not quite 'human' yet – merely 'monsters' wearing human masks.

Can you describe the technicalities of translating your inspiration into form?

Once you start, you cannot make any mistakes, because it would be impossible to correct them. So I make a sketch first. Actually I don't call it a sketch, I call it a design. Because I am searching for a specific form, I don't bother colouring in the tones as one would do in a formal sketch. For instance, in one of the commissioned projects, I'm thinking about combining the form of a bird with a flower. I came up with the idea based on the Bird-of-paradise. It's a simple, small design. So this is where I start.

How do you translate your idea from this small design into something as big as this? Do you need accurate measurements?

No. I just work intuitively. Let's say, I know that I want it to be about eight feet. So I just start working on the frame with that in mind. It doesn't always turn out exactly as how I first imagined it. But as I measure with my eyes and not with the measuring tape, so that's how it is. I am thinking 'small', but very often the work turns out to be a lot bigger than I'd anticipated [laughs].

Uncompleted woodcarving from the raintree felled in front of the studio in 1998.

Pahlawan, 2017. Stainless steel wire frame with bronze and mild steel.

Do you use the same process for your metal sculptures?

Yes, I also make a rough design. Then I start with a metal frame. For instance, in my current project, I've been working on the frame for two months. I can't afford to make any mistakes and I don't correct them. I just make sure that I get it right the first time. So the whole creative process takes time.

How long would you take to complete the bigger sculptures (measuring around 10 feet)?

About four years. For the bigger works, I was actually working on five artworks at the same time. Sometimes when I begin to feel weary, working constantly on the same thing, I switch to the next artwork and proceed on that one instead. So, in four years I produced about five of these.

Notes

1   Traditional Malay dagger characterized by its unique wavy, double-edged damascene blade and pistol-grip handle.

2   ITM is *Institut Teknologi MARA* (MARA Institute of Technology), now Universiti Teknologi MARA (UiTM), or the MARA University of Technology.

3   Pena (National Writer's Association) was established in 1961. At the end of 1996, it moved to its current location, a bungalow on Jalan Dewan Bahasa, and was renamed Rumah Pena (Pena House). Baha Zain who was deputy director (1992–2004) and then director (2004–2010), envisioned it as a creative hub

where writers, dramatists, musicians and artists could congregate. Collaborative efforts in the past had resulted in exhibitions like Manifestasi Dua Seni I (1970) and II (1971) at Dewan Bahasa dan Pustaka. After Baha Zain left as director, Studio Pena gradually found it difficult to sustain its activities without institutional support. However, artists like Mad, Mansoor and Fauzi continue to persevere despite these challenges, by keeping the door open to young artists.

4   Sutung Umar RS (1948–2016), the secretary-general of Rumah Pena, was a writer and poet. He worked as an editor with Dewan Bahasa dan Pustaka's magazine group and *Berita Harian*.

5   *Lansium parasiticum*, also called *duku* in Malay.

6   The late Tengku Ibrahim bin Tengku Wook, Adiguru Kraf Ukiran Halus Persenjataan (master craftsperson for fine weaponry).

7   Haji Wan Su bin Othman, *Adiguru Kraf Ukiran Kayu* (master craftsperson for fine woodcarving).

8   *Dewan Bandaraya Kuala Lumpur* (Kuala Lumpur City Hall).

9   The Rain Tree (*Samanea saman*) is called the *Pokok Pukul Lima* (Five O'Clock Tree) in Malay, because its leaves start folding up about one and a half hours before sunset, and unfold again at around the same time before sunrise – closely corresponding to 5 p.m. and 5 a.m. in this region. The same occurs whenever it rains, leading to its common name in English.

10 Chengal (*Neobalanocarpus heimii*), a weather-resistant tropical hardwood ideal for building, or outdoor furniture or sculpture works.

11 Angsana (*Pterocarpus indicus*), a popular roadside tree in Malaysia.

12 The *kumbang bubuk kayu* is the Malay term for the Powderpost beetle (*Lyctoxylon dentatum*) which is considered a highly destructive pest of wood products.

13 The Pará rubber tree (*Hevea brasiliensis*), a medium density tropical hardwood typically grown in the numerous rubber plantations within this region.

NOOR MAHNUN MOHAMAD
THE RELENTLESS PURSUIT OF ENDURING BEAUTY

Anum, as she is known within local art circles, is a painter, printmaker and curator. Beginning her career with oils as her primary medium, she has since delved into paper works using pencils and watercolours, as well as intaglio printmaking processes, such as etching and mezzotint. More recently, she has also been curating art shows for non-profit organisations and charitable causes. No matter what medium she employs, there seems to be a common thread that is discernible in all her works – a sensual appreciation for the rhythms of everyday ritual and the often-unnoticed textures of ordinary objects. Such sensibilities have been cultivated from her childhood in Kelantan, where the leisurely pace and quietude of *kampung* (village) life invites one to consider and enjoy simple pleasures.

Growing up in Pasir Puteh, she recalls that it was common for every household to have a plot of *sawah padi* (paddy field) beside the house, and to have a threshing ground to separate the grain from the husks which would then be fed to the chickens. Buffaloes wallowing in mud baths formed a common backdrop. Bathing by the *perigi* (well) at a certain time of the day is a communal routine no longer practised today. Such practices instilled a sense of awareness of one's own circadian rhythms and their relationship to the inherent rhythms in nature and culture. Thus, her work often reflects an underlying sensitivity to such connections, even as she moved to vastly different working environments in Germany, America and back in Malaysia.

Having worked as a curator at Valentine Willie Fine Art, a manager at Rimbun Dahan Arts Centre and a lecturer at various local universities, Anum has more recently freelanced as a curator for non-profit organisations like the Malaysian Aids Foundation and Sisters in Islam. Her work has so far commanded the highest price of any female artist in Malaysia. She has a predilection towards traditional methods that necessitate a mature sense for material and a disciplined attitude towards art making, striving for excellence in every detail.

At the Hochschule für Bildende Künste, Germany, she learned a technique of oil painting which requires the patient and thoughtful mixing and layering of paint. She observes that while many people may not regard traditional oil painting as mixed media, the fact is, oil painters work with different types of pigments, adhesives, resins and surfaces. The exploration of different formulations of oil paint for instance, determines not only its longevity, but also its ability to hold together without cracking, and without losing its transparency and luminosity of colour. Anum is attracted to the overall process of oil painting, which demands a long-drawn-out process of building the painting in layers.

Anum working on a current project.

In her watercolour and pencil works, she creates intricate patterned surfaces by taking pains to draft out a grid. In printmaking, she discovered a love for etching and mezzotint, which demand meticulous planning and experimentation to achieve the right tonal values. Her residency in Florence, Italy, for instance, was at Il Bisonte, a school well-known for upholding traditional principles in printmaking, valuing manual handiwork over short-cuts achieved with mechanised tools. For Anum, such preparatory work is not only a labour of love, but part and parcel of her art.

This unhurried approach is consistent with her temperament and is borne out of the need to capture the less visible qualities of being – physiological sensations, abstract thoughts, or fleeting emotions. The choice of subject matter is based on her daily encounters with such sensations. She tries to capture the transient as well as the enduring patterns in one's daily habits. Her still life paintings do not represent mere objects, but seem to refer more to subjective states of being. A random thought, a poem, a spoken word, a scent, a texture – all become catalysts for ideas that evolve into different series of works. In this post-formalist age, where form (and beauty) no longer captivates the interest of many contemporary artists, and current subject matter all too often includes what many consider ordinary or mundane, Anum uncompromisingly declares that art can and should be about beauty. Her artworks, thus, serve to implore us to look a little longer and a little deeper at beauty easily missed – the beauty expressed in action, emotion and thought.

GROWING UP

Can you tell us how growing up in Kelantan has made an impact on what you love to do today?

Yes, actually. I used to watch my grandmother arrange her fishing gear; she had a certain way of doing it so that people won't step over it. She made her own mattresses as well… She also weaved *mengkuang* (screwpine leaf)[1] mats and sewed her own *baju* (clothes). She taught me how to hem. Of course, I was her favourite granddaughter [laughs]. She has a lot of land and also plants her own garden. So, I think I appreciated her daily rituals, and the rhythm of life back then.

When I went back to Kelantan again recently, I realised that that there has been a shift, a change in the way people live. This is inevitable of course, but I miss the rhythms that I felt there, when I grew up. I think that a lot of what I do today tries to capture a certain rhythm… through textures and patterns and through different objects in my still life works.

Postcard from Tumpat, 2016. Oil on linen.
THE EDGE GALERIE

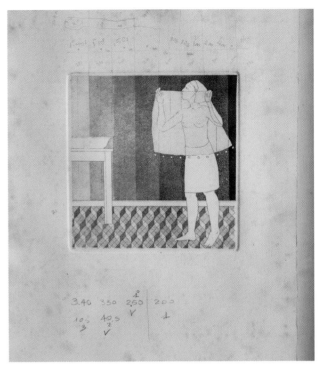

I learnt watercolour from my father who was a teacher. He taught me and my siblings. We would paint during the weekends. At that time, I thought that it was normal, I thought everyone did that, but when I went to school, I realized that I was probably the only one doing watercolour. My mother, too, was very creative. I remember that she would always create unique birthday cakes for us. Like a cake with the 'lid' open, or a family of rabbits made of jelly, rather than something out of a mould!

LEARNING PROCESS

Tell me something about your art education overseas and how that has shaped your learning.

Actually, I was already painting before I went to art school. I had my sketchbook with me all the time and I was painting all kinds of things. So, when I heard about this school (Braunschweig University of Art), I already had my portfolio. With that, I got accepted to sit for the entrance exam.

I was in Professor Arwed D. Gorella's class after the foundation year. He was excellent; the way he critiqued me was very constructive. He would say, 'Oh, I think you should look at this painter,' and I would go to the library and select the artist's monograph. Even now, I always refer to different artists – at the moment, they are Agnes Martin, Stefan Balkenhol, Ellsworth Kelly, David Hockney and Vija Celmins.

Can you tell me about your experience learning printmaking in Italy?

In 2003, I was awarded an Italian Government Scholarship to study printmaking in Florence at the International School of Print and Graphic Il Bisonte for 6 months. That school was internationally very well-known for printmaking. And I was impressed with how everything was done manually and treated with such care and sensitivity. For example, the master who demonstrated how to ink a plate would come in his crisp white linen shirt, and at the end of the day, it remained spotless.

You also received a Nippon foundation grant to do research on Japanese handmade papers. Can you tell us about your trip?

I visited the independent handmade paper makers in 2012. There was about maybe 130 of them in the Tosa province on Shinkoku island. I was taken around to visit paper factories and museums, where I saw how papers were handmade from start to finish.

Left: *Am Abend* (Evening), 1993. Oil on canvas. Completed while Anum was studying in Germany. 'During my studies, I was researching the frescoes of Braunschweig Cathedral, particularly the dance of Salome, and the symbolic use of drapery in such paintings. I started to use the motif of the veil to explore the idea of temptation. Since then it has become a recurring motif.' In 2018, *Am Abend* was sold for RM236,000 at the Henry Butcher Art Auction in Kuala Lumpur (2018).
ANUM

Right: A proof with written notes of the etching process to keep track of the duration the plate is bitten by acid (or stays in the acid bath).

Top: Besides a few pieces of furniture, the studio is kept bare so that the works can be arranged on the ground and on the wall. All are worked on simultaneously throughout the entire painting process, which lasts about six months.

Traditional paper craftsmen still practise this 1000-year-old, labour-intensive process of creating handmade paper by growing trees like mulberry or *gampi*, before harvesting the bark, boiling, rinsing, beating and cleaning out its impurities. For me, besides the beauty of the paper itself, the intensity of labour is part of the appeal of handmade paper. It makes one appreciate the patience and labour it takes to bring something to refinement. A lot of this refinement is lost today, but this is what I want to attain in my work.

SPACE AND PLACE

You've worked in different studios. How does it influence the way you work?

Nowadays I don't go out very often, especially because my studio is now in the same building as my apartment. I find it liberating to be in a constrained space… a kind of self-imposed privacy. I think it depends on the size of the studio. It helps if it's big, because I have a lot of stuff and books. I also need storage space for my artworks. In my previous studio, I also had a big space which

was a living room where I used to do work. At first, it was good, but I didn't produce much work there, though I cannot explain why. I like this [current] space because I love the surroundings here. It's very quiet and there's a great window view. I have a few things that I like to keep with me in the studio – the owl and the pussycat 'masks'. Both sort of 'watch over' me at work and keep me company.

How were your studio spaces overseas set up?

It was very different during my time in Germany. We worked in a factory which had been converted into several large studios. I was allocated a 'corner lot' by the window that offered a view to small gardens. It was quite an ideal studio space.

Most art schools would have an open day, which we would try to attend. During our studio open day, we would either set it up like an exhibition or a work-in-progress studio situation.

We would curate everything from the storage area to the work area.

CURRENT PRACTICE

What have you been working on recently?

I'm now working on a book project. It's a story called *The Very Clever King of Lombok*, by Dina Zaman. So, I've done a little mock-up of the book and am planning a trip to Lombok to do some research about the flora and fauna. I am very interested to know more about the Wallace line and the naturalist Alfred Russell Wallace, who wrote *The Malay Archipelago*.

I've also been doing a series of works on paper for an upcoming solo exhibition at The Edge Galerie.

With my paper works, I like to keep it as minimal as possible. And I enjoy the whole process of doing it. It's tedious and laborious, but that's precisely what I love about it. It's like how I love ironing, cleaning or putting things in order [laughs].

I have also been curating several art shows recently. I enjoy curating, and find that in many ways, I use the same skill set, whether I'm creating art or curating. Because when you curate, you need time management and organisational skills.

In the studio: Natural light is enjoyed throughout the day, the windows open up to a view of the hills and the busyness of the city is momentarily forgotten.

Two paintings showing various stages of work in progress. Colours are built up in a gradual process of layering. This is crucial to achieve a translucent quality in oil, richness in texture, and depth in colour.

MATERIALS AND TOOLS

Can you take us through the process of how you made your own paints as a student?

Of course, but I didn't make my own pigment, otherwise I would have had to go to Elba Island just to get red ochre, or to Afghanistan or Iran to get lapis lazuli [laughs]. There's a very good pigment source called Kremer Pigmente, so I bought pigment in powdered form and mixed it with linseed oil, and then with dammar varnish.

Now, I use Schminke oil paints from the tube, which have the consistency that's just right for me. When I paint, I use dammar varnish in each layer, but I have to be careful. If I put too much, it cracks. You need just enough linseed oil to hold it together. So basically, you need to know a bit of chemistry. The first few layers have more turpentine, the next few layers will be oilier. For the last part, I wait for it to dry for several months before I put on the dammar varnish (either glossy or matte).

Where do you currently source for your art materials?

I buy Schmincke oil paints from Nanyang Art Supplies in Penang and art materials from Straits Commercial in Singapore. The bristle brushes are from Korea. I go to Art Friend[2] for the Arches watercolour paper.

I prefer linen for my canvas as it is stronger, and I like the texture better. Usually, the bigger the painting, the rougher the texture of the surface should be. You want the paint to sit in between the weave of the linen.

That's why I use linen because it has a better weave and texture. Linen is also much more durable. Since I usually spend a long time on a painting, if it tears, I'd be like *aarrgh!* but if there's a dent, I can just spray water from the back of the canvas, it will stretch itself back.

Are there any materials you use which are hard to source?

Balsam turpentine. There are two basic types of turpentine. The industrial turpentine and the other one made from balsam (the resin or sap of certain trees and shrubs) which I prefer because it doesn't make me sick. I love the smell of turpentine, but industrial turpentine makes me nauseated. So, I bought a lot of it the last time, but now I can't get it in Malaysia anymore. It's maddening because I've been using these materials for so long. It's part of the reason I moved to paper works.

For watercolours, I like using Arches or Waterford paper. I also like egg tempera, but I cannot use it here because the cockroaches love it. It's like biscuits for them [laughs].

So, I really need to adapt my work methods and materials according to different climate and places.

With printmaking, for example, my problem is finding a suitable press to work with. But I'm actually exploring some other alternatives right now in terms of getting access to a good printing press, and also doing some research on printing papers. So that when the time is right, I will have the right accommodation and materials to do printmaking.

Left: When working with oil on linen, Anum begins with a rusty coloured base coat which is then left to dry before applying subsequent layers of paint.

Right: Brushes bought over the years come from various travels, roughly sorted on a trolley.

WORKING PROCESS

Can you describe your typical day?

I wake up quite early, somehow. For whatever reasons, I wake up practically at 5 a.m. and then I'm out of bed. Sometimes I stay in my pyjamas and just start working. At around 11:30 a.m. every day, I cook lunch, and then around 4:30pm, I stop to take a tea break. Sometimes I read. I am currently reading Goethe's *Schönste Gedichte*, and *The Best Australian Poems* (2008). On a busy day, I continue working till 3 a.m. in the morning.

You are known for your traditional/classical methods in painting. Tell us about this process.

Well, when you talk about the painting process, you need to be familiar with the anatomy of the oil painting. First, you start with the support, which is the strainer or the stretcher. In Germany, we were taught to make our own, so I would stretch the canvas myself then, but now I get the framer to do it. When I was a student, I made the 'size'[3] for my canvas using rabbit skin glue. Then, I mixed my own primer for the sized canvas, which is usually made out of plaster of Paris, Titanium White, mixed with sizing and linseed oil.

Now, I buy ready-made, prepared canvas or linen, and my framer will stretch it according to the size that I want. So, by doing this, I save time. Usually, I buy it in bulk, two to three times a year. So, I have all this canvas in my studio waiting.

As a student, I referred to *Doerner*.[4] It's a really good book, and I experimented with different ratios to come up with a consistency that suits me.

How do you choose your subject matter?

Sometimes, it comes randomly. As I'm going about reading or looking at something, a word would trigger something. So, my sketchbook is always with me and most of the drawings are very quick ones, just to capture the idea before it goes away... The imagination is fertile, but these thoughts and sensations can be very fleeting… and with one idea giving birth to another.

'Fish Head,' 2017, 30.5 x 30cm, 20 x 30cm (Diptych), Oil on Linen.

THE EDGE GALERIE

The other day, I was just thinking about my upcoming solo exhibition. I wanted to paint a still life of an orchid, so I bought one. But it died, so I bought another one, then I thought: 'How apt, because "still life" is *natura morta* in Italian, meaning "dead nature" [laughs].' So this is how some of the ideas develop.

Notes

1   Mengkuang, screwpine leaf, (*Pandanus odoratissimus*).

2   Art Friend is an art supply chain available in Singapore, Malaysia and Vietnam.

3   'Sizing' a canvas is the application of a substance to reduce the absorbency of the painting surface and stop the paint from having direct contact with the surface fibres, thereby protecting the canvas from the acidity of linseed oil.

4   Max Doerner was a German painter who authored *The Materials of the Artists and their Use in Painting* (1984). His book details the types of materials used in painting from the Renaissance period up to the present day.

SHARON CHIN
TRANSFORMATIVE SPACES

Sharon is a multimedia artist who draws, paints, performs and writes. Her art includes a host of playful experiments in the form of installations, performance art, zines, paintings, prints and found objects. Whether in action or in print, her works are marked by an immediate frankness and affability that is hard to ignore. It carries the kind of visual appeal that fuses the familiar and the unexpected, in a way that demands our contemplation. Her artworks invite us, as viewers, to examine ourselves and our daily actions and see how they contribute to collective behaviour and social norms. In urban environments where apathy and self-interest often dominate communal interests, her work is a balm against increasing cynicism and indifference.

For Sharon, art is both personal and social. Her art practice is drawn from her personal journeys in life but is always related to the social aspects of living within a community. In the same way, she asks her audiences to also think critically about their personal motivations and experience, and how these are extrapolated to their larger social spheres. For instance, in *Mandi Bunga*[1] (2013) she invited audiences to ponder over questions like 'What does it mean to do something alone?', 'What does it mean to do something together?' and 'How can we be ourselves with others?' *Mandi Bunga* was an art performance that brought 100 participants out onto the lawn of the Singapore Art Museum, who then clad themselves in yellow sarongs and bathed themselves in a collective cleansing act. Prior to the performance, drawings were made to encourage participation, and workshops were held to personalize the sarongs to be worn on the day. Documentation then took the form of videos with shots taken by the audience themselves, as well as a zine published to explain her motives. The performance and the interaction were deliberately planned to help the audience connect in specific ways.

Even within the practice of drawing, Sharon is critical of her approach and process. She contends that drawing is personal and compares it to the way we write or speak. The act of drawing has become, for her, so much more than a way of representing objects or nature; it has become a way of thinking or learning about them, which serves to ground her other multimedia works. In a publication called *Draw, Make, Create*[2] published by the Queensland Art Gallery, Sharon drew activity pages for kids, based on her local area in Port Dickson and invited kids to make a newspaper about their own neighbourhoods. Such a deceptively simple project design stemmed from her own sense of place and was ingeniously employed to encourage children to relate to the spaces they inhabit. Larger interests about the sense of place were addressed as a contemporary social phenomenon.

As an art writer, Sharon writes about her own work as well as the work of her friends.

A spacious high-ceiling 1970s bungalow affords a laid-back work space in the coastal town of Port Dickson.

She acknowledges the difficulties of language in describing artistic impulses or describing artistic practice. Therefore, she uses her writing as a way to speak less formally about art, so that the space between the artist and the audience might be bridged. Through her weblogs,[3] her writing complements her art by clarifying abstract thoughts and instinctive decisions throughout the process of art creation.

Her efforts to make art more accessible to the public is also evident in her presentation of art itself. She is mindful in creating environments where people can let go of formalities and momentarily forget that they are in a museum or gallery. She remarks that the awareness of the museum and gallery space often invokes a kind of self-consciousness that dictates the way people engage with art in manners that limit their enjoyment of art, such as not touching the art exhibits or not talking to the person next to you. So, the presentation of her artwork transforms the formal spaces of the gallery into casual settings that break this convention and help people interact more meaningfully with the work and the artist.

At the end of the day, Sharon's works always combine the element of play with a serious desire to make positive changes to the places we live in. She says, art seduces with the form. It inspires us to think differently and has the potential to transform the way we connect with people, places or nature. Her work is thus grounded in her personal struggles and victories, which become the platform for an authentic voice for change.

GROWING UP

Can you remember your first exposure to art?

Books. Pictures books. I have a strong memory of activity books my mom made for me when I was still in primary school. My mother lectured at University Malaya and she taught English. Sometimes, while I waited for her, she would make these worksheets for her students. On an A4 piece of paper, she would cut out comic strips from the newspaper, then she would have a section where you have to 'complete this story' or 'complete this sentence'…. there would be little games. She left me in her office while she taught, and she would make the activity sheets for me as well.

To this day, I have this 'activity book' approach – a way of entertaining yourself for five hours, or a way of thinking through a problem. You're left to yourself. There's no iPad, you've just gotta do things until mom comes back!

It's the same thing with art. You just spend time 'doing stuff'. In a way, you need to be bored in order to make things. I think, if you're not bored, it becomes hard to create.

SPACE AND PLACE

Tell us about your current space.

This place (Port Dickson) is my partner's childhood home. He (Zedeck Siew) and his family moved to KL 15 years ago. But he grew up here, and they never sold this house. It was empty for 10 years. So, we decided to move here.

When we first moved here, Zedeck was like, 'Eh, you just use the living room hall *lah*'. I felt, 'Oh, but it's not fair to you, because then I'll be taking over the hall.' But when I had my studio at the back, this space wasn't being used. And that room was becoming too small. So, we would come out sometimes and work here together, and it's so much better. Previously, the centre was empty and we were off in our own rooms, doing our own thing. Yeah, not so fun. Now it has become the heart of the home. And the light here is great.

What kind of changes have you experienced since moving here?

A city like KL wasn't conducive for me and for him (as a writer). Even though we were busier than ever, I felt I was moving further and further away from what I really wanted to do. I was not happy, and I wasn't quite sure why. I felt like I wasn't clear in terms of direction, the thoughts and ideas [in my work] weren't clear.

I would say that the biggest change was and is, my relationship with time. It wasn't drastic but it was profound. I found that I wasn't finishing my thoughts [when I was in the city]. I was so bound by projects and project deadlines, that the focus was always on fulfilling the briefs of the project. 'Oh, you're part of this group show.' It's almost like you are making work to its [preconceived] specifications. That kind of work crept up on me, and I realised that I was the content provider for the curator or anybody who was setting the agenda, the programme.

When I moved here, I didn't make art for about two years. It was hard, really hard… I just couldn't. There was a mini existential crisis. I think it's because I had forgotten how to make art without the project structure, without the deadline and the commission – 'Oh without that, will I still continue to make art?', 'Who am I?', that kind of thing.

One day, I remembered thinking, 'I'll just start drawing again.' From then on, my process changed. Now, I would say that I'm ahead of any agenda, I know what art I want to make and what's important to me. So, when people ask me to be a part of their project, it's very clear what my position is on most things and I also feel free to say 'no'.

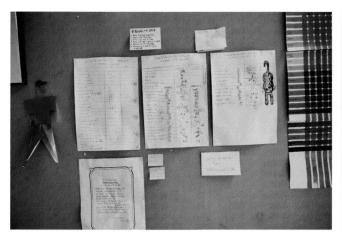

Sharon and Zedeck on how they keep their focus when working on a long project: 'There's just so much drawing to be done, so Zedeck made me this chart. After finishing each one, you get a cat doodle. It's like for kindergarten kids! But this is how we get out of work.'

A children's activity sheet featuring plants, furry friends and other encounters in Taman Toh Kee Kah (Sharon's neighbourhood in Port Dickson), published in *Draw, Make, Create*.

Small pleasures: plants and weeds cut from the garden inspire drawings and prints.

How does being closer to nature impact your work?

This [place] isn't even rural, it is semi-urban – but the difference is great! How many animals we interact with every day [in this place] is amazing compared to KL and PJ.

We have tree frogs, they will come out in the evening and live in the house. Once a year, we'll get a giant centipede in here. It's about this [indicates approximately 12 inches] big. There are monkeys, a *musang* (palm civet) who comes to eat the *nangka* (jackfruit), and so many kinds of birds and all the different bugs.

Being with nature or living with animals changes how I think. The artwork becomes less human-centric. Less about human history, national history or human identity, but instead it becomes wider. Without nature, there's no culture, no history, no art, and no livelihood. Everything comes from the earth and we're coming to a point where we're taking so much for granted. It's great to live here, and to be able to experience this.

We're really lucky, the only way our life works is because we don't have to pay rent. Without the rental burden, so much is possible… so, so much.

That's why, one thing I argue for is that if you want to promote the arts, forget about grants, forget about these programmes, *et cetera*. Offer housing instead. It all comes down to economy because [for example] the state [government], when they think about encouraging artistic activity, it's usually too programmatic, whereas what you want to

do is let the artists get on with it. You want to facilitate the artist, let the artist lead the content.

What about residencies?

The thing about artist residencies is that you live somewhere else. One of the ideas I have is a local neighbourhood residency program. Basically, it's another way of subsidising housing for artists. The artist does the residency where they live. Because, instead of taking the artist out and putting them somewhere that is alien, you are getting the artist to interact with the community. So, the work that artists do is about their surroundings and the people in their surroundings. It's less centralised. But I don't know whether other artists want that. I mean, artists want careers, and going to an artist residency [is] glamorous.

LEARNING PROCESS

When you first graduated, did you actually do what you wanted to do?

In my first solo show, I did exactly what I wanted. That was 100% me …that was in 2005. Following that – if I can critique myself – I would say that the work was not so resolved… it was just not so strong.

Can you talk about how blogging has shaped your work?

I started a website when I came here. I realised that if I don't put something out there, I'm just not going to exist, because the [art] center is in KL. So, I started using the internet in a more intentional way, as a tool instead of just consuming, like surfing the net or using Facebook. It helped me speak about my own work in a different way. I started to question the way we use language around exhibitions, such as the press statement and the artist statement. Why is it so formal? And how is that language interfacing with an audience or a public? It wasn't just regarding how my work was written about, it was also about how I was writing and how the work was being presented in a gallery.

I started to write about art differently, not just about my own work but about my friends' as well. My writing became more straightforward, using the straightforward voice like speaking, and being also more, I would say, subjective and emotional. I realised that people talk about art in a way that is so distanced. Blogging definitely helped me to work around that.

I have dreaded the whole exhibition structure ever since my first show, I have hated openings, whether my own or other peoples'. I started thinking about why I dread it so much. I thought, 'Oh, my god, does it mean that people who come to my openings feel the way I do? That's terrible!' I started to think about the 'self-accepted' structure of the exhibition, which includes the opening, and to see how I could change that.

Can you give an example from one of your shows?

My first solo show after being here [Port Dickson] was in 2013 and I held it at a friend's gig space, *Merdekarya* in PJ. This was the *Rumpai* (Weeds) series [weeds painted on political flags].[4] We had open mic night and a colouring table where people could doodle and do crafts. So, the work – which is a serious work – became more like a backdrop; it created the setting for people to come together. I liked it that people came to hang out and the work is just there. That changed how people related to the art.

When you started out, did you have a mentor to help you with your art practice?

My first and only mentor was Chee Sek Thim.[5] He gave me my first solo show when I came back from overseas. I had reverse culture shock, full of angst and nervous energy. He was encouraging, but tough-minded.

[But] the mentoring relationship was one of authority, so it's not useful for me now. Whereas if we talk and work together on something regardless of age or how much we know, I would find that a more fruitful kind of relationship. But Sek Thim was a mentor that I needed when I started out.

Can you talk about how drawing has become an essential artistic process?

Since moving here, my relationship with drawing [has changed]. In art school, I was in the sculpture department; my work was not drawing-based. I had this idea in my head that I don't know how to draw.

When locals meet me, the first thing they will say is, 'Oh you're an artist, right? Can you draw this for me? Can you draw that for me?' So, it's like, 'Okay Sharon, you better learn to draw.' That was in reaction to the local requirements of what people think an artist is.

Around that time, I was also looking at this artist, Lynda Barry. Two of her books made a huge impression on me.[6] One is about drawing and making pictures, and another is about writing. It's not really about skill or making 'good' drawings, but how the process of drawing can help you think and see.

There's no such thing as a good or bad drawing. Some really good drawings that are technically beautiful can look kind of dead. Think about why we love children's drawings – because there's that freedom of line, there's spontaneity. You don't try to make that line perfect. It's as individual as your thumbprint.

CURRENT PRACTICE

Tell us about your current book project with Zedeck Siew.

This will be his first published book. The images I produce are based on his stories. The whole book project is quite epic because there are 50 animal stories and 25 plant stories. It's been two years running (since 2015), as I've been working on it in batches. I did a show half-way through: an in-progress show on the animal prints, at Run Amok, in Penang.

This kind of a long, sustained work is something quite new to me. I have not experienced [working at] just producing images – sitting in a studio and producing the works. The art helps to finance the book.

Sharon talking to fellow artist Candice Ng, during the set-up of 'Between States' at OUR ArtProjects, KL. Her work entitled, 'Politics' (2011–Current), comprises 5 jackets hung on chairs around a table in a casual set-up that invites viewers to sit down and have a conversation about the work.

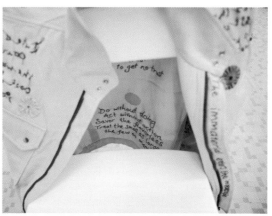

'Do without doing. Act without action. Savour the flavorless. Treat the small as large, the few as many.' Lao Tzu's words of wisdom and other statements sewn on the insides of this jacket, a connotation of how external appearances only hint at the complex personal philosophies we each carry inside.

Above: Sharon sewing yellow and red threads across a denim jacket based on *Rumpai* (Weeds).

Bottom, right: Denim jacket based on *Mandi Bunga* is draped over a chair in *Politics* (2011–Current).

We are very excited about the book because it means that the artworks will be distributed to different kinds of audiences. It will be presented in book form and will also exist as art objects. There will be 50 designs and each one will be printed 20 times.

In your current work for 'Between States' (2017), do you think about ways of getting your audience to think about a certain issue? Or is this work your way of figuring it out for yourself?

It's both. The subject that I'm interested in right now, is local council politics – quite a banal subject for most people. The project is for me to learn about it because I feel it's important. Then, by presenting it in an artwork, it also helps people to understand it... I think art seduces by the form.

I started to use these punk jackets: the idea being, wearing your politics on your sleeve! This particular one has patches that I've collected over time from other artists and friends.

The rest of the jackets are based on my previous work like *Mandi Bunga, Bersih 2.0, Rumpai*, and Port Dickson.

The jacket that's about Port Dickson is based on the politics of the everyday; like open burning, trash collection or how we deal with pollution. It's about what it means to live away from the capital as opposed to the drama and spectacle of party politics that dominates much of current affairs in the capital. Sometimes these tend to overshadow the everyday stuff, which is not being taken care of.

When you are in the midst of producing the work, do you think about who is going to buy the work or how are they going to put it up in their gallery?

Yeah, I do. Like for my lino prints, the paper is very important. When we made the editions, we only framed one set. While, for the rest of the edition of prints, I just covered [them up] in plastic. People who have bought it have sent me pictures of the artworks in their house. Some frame it, and some people masking-tape it to the wall. I love that, actually – [the fact that] it is not too precious. It's good if people don't need to frame something up and can still enjoy the artwork. Like the *Weeds* artwork, you can just stick it to the wall with Blu Tack,[7] or fold it up like a piece of cloth and look at it when you want to.

MATERIALS AND TOOLS

What particular tools do you use for your lino work?

I use a 'baren', which I ordered from Japan. It's a traditional printmaking tool that's able to create more pressure. I've done it with a wooden spoon too, but you can't get the density. Inside [the baren] is a coil, like a twisted cord, and that's how it transfers the force from the arm down. This one is only a lower- to medium-quality baren. The best quality barens cost like 1,000 dollars, but those are great, those are for master woodcutters.

Yes. It's all about the weight and the transference of the force of the arm onto the paper. As for the really expensive ones, the cord will be wound very tightly. They are traditionally made from bamboo fibre.

How far do you go to search for the materials? Or do you try to use whatever is in front of you?

Yeah, more and more lately, I just use what's in front of me. The paper I get from Thailand. It's mulberry paper, so it's very good for printmaking. I like that it's from Thailand and not further away, like the Italian or the Japanese papers. Things that are made here are more suited to our climate, and inexpensive.

One of my dreams is to go make a better baren, then Malaysians can have their own [locally-made baren] because you can use [local materials such as] banana fibre. We have a lot of bamboo as well, so perhaps that is another option.

In terms of basic art materials, do you consistently use the same types or brands?

Yeah, that's one thing that is quite consistent. I often revert back to school quality art

Sharon's basic set of lino-cutting tools.

Sharon Chin, *Mandi Bunga*, 2013, Singapore Biennale.
SHIRLEY NG

Mandi Bunga drawings
SHARON CHIN

materials. Especially when I'm stuck, I find that I always go back to that exercise book paper, or Buncho[8] – the things that I grew up with.

So, I have a mix of high-end and low-end materials. The professional stuff, and this kind of 'back-to-school' quality Chinese paint. Some people keep very beautiful sketch books but I cannot; it's always been exercise book paper. I do use the professional stuff, but when I feel stuck, I come back to this. For some reason, it allows me to let go. Just forget that you are a so-called professional artist.

WORKING PROCESS

Can you describe your typical day?

A typical day would be… I wake up quite early and I have a very short yoga stretching routine. I have to do it, otherwise the day hasn't started. Sometimes I miss it and the whole day doesn't feel quite right. Then I get down to work. Because I'm working on

this book project where I need to do many illustrations and prints… it is just one after the other, so there is quite a routine at the moment, and probably for another two months. It's really [keeping at it] one by one, and the days are measured like that. Yeah, the break is lunch and dinner and then I do *muay thai*. So, eat, sleep, *muay thai*, and do this.

In a usual work process, how long do you take to conceptualise the work before you actually start working?

It depends. For example, my process has really changed since I moved here. The first work I started making after moving here was the *Weeds* work. I would say that that process was more organic.

One day I started drawing the weeds in my garden and it was just a daily practice; every day I would draw one weed. At that time, they started putting up flags for the elections. Every time I see one, I will *curi* (steal it). I was doing that for 'don't know why', and 'don't know how long', until I ended up with a stockpile of flags.

One day, I was like, 'Oh, hey! I'm going to try painting on the flag.' That became a body of work. It was really about the process of responding to my surroundings and what I was feeling, thinking and reading.

Whereas in *Mandi Bunga*, which was this big performance I did in Singapore in 2013, I had thought of the idea even before they asked me to join the show. That came out of participating in Bersih.[9] I had already written a proposal and it was ready for an opportunity.

In your current works for the story book, would you do any research about the animals you are going to illustrate?

In this case, I mostly work off the story. For example, when I drew this cannabis pattern – in my mind, I already know what a marijuana plant looks like, so if I research too much, I feel like the image begins to [have a] lifeless quality. It could be technically very good when you have a reference image in front of you, but the image can sometimes miss the spontaneity.

And it's the same with *Mandi Bunga*. I consciously resisted researching about different practices all over the world. I grew up with the tradition, like my grandma and my dad, where after going to the funeral, you *mandi bunga*. So, I stuck to that. I know that it is practiced in the Malay culture, Indian culture, Orang Asal[10] culture, and that's enough. That's all I need to know. What's important in that work was not really the information but how it was carried out.

That's very interesting to know. Previously, you did do a lot more research?

Yes. In fact, it was heavily researched. I was following a tradition. I think there's a tradition in Malaysia of research-based work… like (Wong) Hoy Cheong's work, many of the more senior artists, I think, research their works a lot, and the works are also quite text-based.

But I started to ask myself, 'Do you need to know the information before you can read the artwork?' The artwork is a kind of text. As an artist, what I'm interested in are the visual aspects of the work. When you look at the artwork, there could be many layers and depths to it, but ultimately, do you have a reaction when you look at the work?

Also, I think nobody likes to say the words …'emotional content', about the artwork. I feel like, today, it's almost embarrassing or seems sentimental to say that. But for me, it's important and it doesn't mean that the work is not intellectual.

Notes

1 The title, *Mandi Bunga*, literally means 'floral baths', referring to the cleansing ritual of bathing with flowers that is performed by many cultures in Malaysia.

2 *Draw, Make, Create* was published by the Children's Art Centre of Queensland Art Gallery, Gallery of Modern Art (QAGOMA), in conjunction with the 8th Asia Pacific Triennial of Contemporary Art in 2015.

3 Sharonchin.com

4 *Rumpai* (Weeds) was produced during the election campaign period before the 13th Malaysian general elections in 2013; it comprised black and white illustrations of weeds painted over flags of the Barisan National and Pakatan Rakyat political parties.

5 Chee Sek Thim is a theatre actor and director as well as the founder of RekaArt Space, established in 2002 in Petaling Jaya, currently located in George Town, Penang.

6 Lynda Barry, 'Picture This', *Montreal: Drawn and Quarterly*, 2010, and Lynda Barry, 'What It Is', *Montreal: Drawn and Quarterly*, 2008.

7 Blu Tack is a popular brand of reusable putty adhesive used to adhere lightweight objects to walls.

8 Buncho is an inexpensive brand of poster colour paints, popular amongst local schoolchildren.

9 Bersih (Clean), short for Gabungan Pilihanraya Bersih dan Adil (Coalition for Clean and Fair Elections), was formed in 2006 by non-governmental organisations. Supporters wear yellow shirts during street demonstrations as a symbol of protest, demanding reforms in the electoral process. Bersih: 2007, Bersih 2.0: 2011, Bersih 3.0: 2012, Bersih 4: 2015, Bersih 5: 2016.

10 Orang Asal is the Malay term for 'original peoples', referring to the diverse indigenous communities in the region.

The illustration is first drawn on paper before being transferred onto a lino sheet, where the design is cut in relief for inking and printing.

ABDUL MANSOOR IBRAHIM
QUIET IMPRESSIONS

Artist printmaker virtuoso Abdul Mansoor relishes working with the medium of print. Although trained in oil painting, printmaking is a medium that, he says, 'carries him a long way.' The long hours and slow preparation invested in composing, carving, engraving, inking and printing are satisfying in ways which he finds absent in painting.

Having trained at Institut Teknologi MARA (ITM) and later at Atelier 17, Paris, during the 1970s, he experienced a period of increasing democratisation of art. Mansoor recalls that while the Atelier remained focused on the technical and formal aspects of print, the waves created by the New York Pop artists could be felt across Europe. Printmaking, vis-à-vis Pop Art, had inadvertently made art accessible to a wider general audience. His own preference for print works may be partly shaped by such developments. He says, 'I appreciate print works as opposed to painting because more people can buy and own original works of art.' Limited edition prints, that run up to 100 editions per plate, enable the creation of more affordable and less exclusive art.

Printmaking has remained Mansoor's medium of choice, whether he is absorbed in the formal aspects of art or concerned about its social functions. He acknowledges that while working in Paris, he had been experimenting mostly with the finer technical aspects of pulling a print. Under the leading voice of the Atelier, William Hayter,[1] he became skilled in the viscosity techniques of lithography and the *contrepoint* methods of composition. He states flatly that his works convey neither his emotional nor spiritual states. Instead, they are simply about the joy of exploring forms and finding those that can capture and sustain the mind's eye.

These forms are not drawn from within but from the physical and visual qualities of nature. In this sense, his approaches to composition are as objective as those of Gestalt proponents who systematically experimented with formal elements to find a universal logic underlying visual perception. In Mansoor's prints, this objectivity is poised against the emotive language of colour and texture. This is evident in his series of collagraphs entitled *Renyuk* (Crumpled), which makes use of actual objects to produce compelling textures.

Nature, as a subject close to his heart, is regarded as an inspiring source for artistic form as well as a source of life itself. Plants, animals and landscapes are preferred to man or man-made objects. Being an intensely private person, he appreciates the impersonal distance that nature as subject matter affords him. Recurring sensorial memories which are fleeting, ambiguous and intangible, easily find their visual articulation in Abstract Expressionism.

Being comfortable with abstraction as a language, he found figuration and all forms

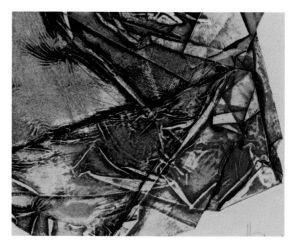

Left: *3 Sequences*, 1980. Etching with viscosity technique.

MANSOOR

Middle: *Renyuk* series. 1981. Collagraph. In a collagraph, actual objects like foil, paper, natural organic material etc. are glued to a board, then inked and printed. This series of collagraph was produced at Studio Anak Alam during the 1980s, where Mansoor was invited to oversee the printing workshop.

Right: Detail of *Renyuk* Series.

of representational art inept. After many years of art practice, however, he submits that abstraction does not satisfy his own personal yearnings to talk about social issues in more concrete ways. He says, 'It was a challenge to relate to the audience because it [my work] was regarded as decoration.' His move towards the *Serangga* (insect) series was partly a response to this issue. The *Serangga* series consists of accurate documentations of the anatomy of insects, which uses insects as metaphors for specific negative social attitudes that pervade contemporary urban society. Mansoor's approach favours the implied and the suggestive over more antagonistic means of social commentary.

As a teacher of printmaking, he accedes that the digital age is already transforming methods of print, enabling the younger generation of printmakers to successfully replicate the effects of manual prints with computer generated works. He disagrees that one should romanticise the manual press as having a higher artistic value than digital presses. The idea that an artwork should bear the mark of the artist's hand, has been long dismissed by contemporary conceptual artists.

Mansoor argues that the value of printmaking lies in the process it offers the artist, rather than an insistence on the 'physical labour' it involves. Being introverted, he takes great pains to create distance from his work. He finds little pleasure in making public appearances in art galleries and seems to value, more highly, the private aspects of art practice. Meaning, for him, is derived from the routine processes of drawing, incising, engraving and printing.

GROWING UP

What were your first exposures to art?

When I was growing up, my eldest brother used to draw and paint a lot. He also bought books on Art History. I used to watch him paint in oil but somehow I didn't mess around with it. But in school, my favourite subject was Art and I was in the Art Club. I also remembered Ms. Chai who was my art teacher. She was very good and really exposed me to the fundamental elements of art, like line and shade, *et cetera*. I was in Kajang High School at the time.

My dad passed away when I was nine. At that time, my brother had just received his Senior Cambridge 'O' level results. He had no choice but to support us. He had to sacrifice his own dreams of being an artist. He went to Maktab Perguruan Sultan Idris,[2] and today he is an art teacher.

Did he influence your decision to become an artist?

Actually, he was surprised when I wanted to enrol in ITM to study art! He said, 'Are you sure this is the course you want to take?' I said, 'Yes', and he said, 'Okay, at least you are carrying my flag' [meaning I was upholding his dream]. Throughout college, he was behind me financially and also gave me moral support. He let me do some of his commissioned works so that I could earn some money. At that time, he would get about RM20 to RM30 per piece, which was considered a lot in those days.

LEARNING PROCESS

Can you remember some of your milestones in your learning process?

My time at ITM was very productive. We had teachers like Piyadasa, Sulaiman Esa, Joseph Tan, Tan Teong Eng and Choong Kam Kow. I spent four years there. The first year was foundation and after that I majored in Printmaking and minored in Painting. I was the first batch of three students to major in Printmaking [in 1975]. Ahmad Khalid Yusoff, Kok Yew Puah and Carol, a visiting lecturer from America was teaching printmaking.

Also, as first year students, I remember being impacted by the New Scene artists[3] who had written a manifesto, and I remember thinking: 'This is how serious art is', that someone would take the trouble to write a manifesto! It was something new for us. They really challenged us in class. They taught us technical skills and, later, conceptual work. The syllabus was based on Bauhaus ideas. I was also very close to the late Kok Yew Puah. He had just returned from Australia and was doing large scale silkscreens. I was really impressed.

What impacted your learning most during your studies in France?

École des Beaux-Arts in France is very traditional and their teaching was typical of academic schools. In fact they tend to hold fast to their artistic traditions. It is surprising but accurate to say that there was more artistic debate happening in the four years I was in ITM, than in the academy in Paris! I think ITM gave me a strong foundation in terms of thinking about art as a subject.

So, in Paris, it was more of the exposure to international artists and being able to see their work 'face-to-face' in the museums that impacted me.

What about your time at Atelier 17 under William Hayter?

The way it was structured at that time, we would go to the academy in the morning and in the evening we would work at the Atelier. So, it was in the Atelier that we learnt how to be *professional* printmakers. They had a very good gallery system, where the students never lacked a so-called market for their works. The art infrastructure was very developed.

Hayter himself was a chemist and he created the 'viscosity printing technique' in printmaking, where different colours can be printed using the same printing plate. This is done by adjusting the ratio of linseed oil with the ink. Inks with different viscosity will repel one another so the colours don't mix. His Atelier was also known for the *contrepoint* method. It's a method of composition that helps you structure the flow of lines and dramatize the composition to hold the attention of the viewer. These are the specific techniques I adopted from the Atelier.

And on my own, I found it very useful to analyse the works of the old masters like Rembrandt and Goya. Or German Expressionists like Kirschner and the Abstract Expressionist, Kandinsky.

SPACE AND PLACE

How did you come about working in Studio Pena?

In 2005, Mad Anuar invited me to join him here. He has a printing press but he needed someone to handle it. So I decided to join them. At that time the National Writer's Association thought that it would be beneficial to work closely together to exchange ideas. As writers and artists, we can work on the same subject but in different media. We had a common interest in creating works of art. I thought it was a good idea.

How do you organise your work space here?

It's kind of an open lab. In the middle is where we do our sketches and talk. But each one of us has our own space: one for ceramics, one for metal welding, one for wood sculpture, one for printing, one for storage. But to tell you the truth, we are looking for a better space in the future because, for printmaking, this space is not ideal. It needs to be closed up and air-conditioned, so that we can leave our works here and they can be secure.

What do you like most about this space?

We are comfortable with this space. Although we are in the KL city centre, you don't feel like it because it is surrounded by trees. That's the beauty of this place. There is no disturbance. It's up to us how long we want to work.

Not all artists pull their own prints, often due to lack of a printing press. Here, Mansoor helps a friend print an etching.

Everyone is welcome to visit us anytime. And we do have students who intern with us, but we don't accept more than two students at a time because this is a small space.

How does sharing the space with this collective shape the way you work?

We have a lot of discussions and we throw different ideas around. This helps me think through my practice. And discussions happen at different levels depending on what you are interested in. Some prefer to talk about technical issues, some about teaching art and some about concepts of art. All these are important and this space is conducive to it. We are very open, we are not selfish.

CURRENT PRACTICE

Tell me about your current project

I recently completed a series of engravings on insects. I worked on it from 2012 to 2016. A friend of mine is an entomologist and a professor in UKM (Universiti Kebangsaan Malaysia). He was doing research on *riang-riang*, or the cicada. In the life cycle of the cicada, the eggs take between 10 and 12 years to hatch. So, rapid deforestation is likely to destroy them. He said to me, 'I can't fight this. It's such a pity.' Still, he managed to find new species along the way. That was how I became interested in these insects. So, in that series I used them as metaphors to comment on social and political issues.

Can you give me an example of an issue you are concerned with?

For example, I wanted to talk about the problem of squatter homes in the city. But I don't want to comment on it too directly because that's not my style. So I used the hermit crab as a metaphor. The hermit crab is viewed as an intruder because it sometimes steals and lives in other animals' shells. So, I titled the work on the hermit crab, *rumah haram* (illegal squatters), as an indirect way of questioning the fact that inhabiting squatter homes is considered illegal (while destroying them is not). In the case of the tick, I titled it as 'bloodsucker'. Likewise, different insects like the cockroach, grasshopper, and dragonfly are used to show different traits of society.

How do you select your subject matter?

I've always tried to portray different aspects of humanity through nature, whether it's landscape, or insects etc. I don't think that has changed even though I've changed my medium. Even when I was working on abstraction, my visual source has always been nature. My works are also expressionistic. But you cannot comment using Abstract Expressionism. So even though I love the subtle approach of expressionism, it was frustrating to find that some people viewed it as mere decoration – it's treated like furniture in a living room.

How did you deal with that challenge?

I struggled with it because it was not my style to do confrontational works. I know a lot of artists who do social commentary work and I support them. I think what they are doing is great, but it is just not me. I am not that type of assertive character. I like a more subtle approach and that is why finally I decided to turn to the depiction of insects as an alternative to more confrontational approaches. I hope the titles will give the audience a clue to what my topic of interest is.

You also switched from lithography and etching to wood engraving. Do you still enjoy the etching process?

Absolutely. There is a beauty to each type of printmaking process. For me printmaking is a process that really carries me a long way. It's not merely about the final product. It's a very technical process. You have to know the chemistry of the ink and the different types of paper. You have to be very meticulous. It's about the discipline and the repetition of the routine that is important to me. That's the beauty of it, because life is all about discipline. It is a thinking process. You have to be disciplined in your thinking process. You can't just jump to the final product or the final chapter.

As a lecturer, how do you teach printmaking to the current generation?

I realise that it is not for everyone. So I wouldn't push my students to do etching if it's not their thing. Traditional methods like these are too slow for them. And perhaps these methods are not meant to last forever. If you try to use old methods to teach the younger generation, you will lose them.

In UiTM,[4] they have their own syllabus and they asked me to teach etching and dry point. But I think the way forward is to move with technology. We are already living in the digital era. We should think about digital printing as a contemporary medium. You no longer need to know silkscreen, for example. You can achieve the same thing digitally. It can be done.

I also think that installation art has become a more relevant art form for today. For my next project, I am considering installation combined with printing as a medium.

I think that, as artists, we have to remain open to possibilities. We must not get stuck in one medium with the use of old machines. We should recognise that art can be produced with any medium, whether copper, wood or paper.

MATERIALS AND TOOLS

Where do you source your wood and what types of wood are suitable for your engraving?

For wood engraving, you need very hard and fine woods such as the *ciku, kemuning, pokok asam jawa*, or *penaga laut*.[5] These types of hard woods are usually used for the hilt of the *keris*[6] or the handle of the *parang*.[7] You need to use the end grain[8]

Basic engravers tools: A four-piece set of burins bought during his early days as a printmaker.

Bottom left: A collection of smaller pieces of wood for engraving, loosely piled on a shelf with various printing inks.

Bottom right: Work space for inking and cleaning plates.

We usually leave it for five years to mature. Then I handsaw the wood into blocks of about one inch thick and use the sander to smoothen it.

Tell me about your tools.

I use the burin because I'm doing very detailed work. The burin is V-shaped and suitable for fine cuts on hard wood. It does take some practice to master. When I first started, I practised everyday for about six months in order to really know the character of the burin. You can produce very linear work with it.

We can also get the machine-shop kind of tools, as long as it's a high-carbon tool. We can always modify that. It's easier for us to buy ready-made, but it's more expensive because a three-piece set of burins may cost about RM300, if it is imported from Australia or Japan. So modifying is a good alternative.

Where do you source your papers?

We have a lot of etching papers especially from Penang. It's much cheaper, I think. I buy in bulk from Penang. Or else, you can import them from Japan. Sometimes we have colleagues working here from America and Japan. When they return, we just ask them to buy some papers.

As for engraving papers we can use *washi*, which is Japanese handmade paper; these are well-tested and made from plant fibres. Or a Chinese handmade paper called Shilu paper; these are different from those used for ink painting.

Tell me about your press.

This press is small scale and produces about 20 inches of print. The length varies according to the length of the print. This machine was originally a latex [rubber] sheeting press. We got help from an engineer friend who modified the machine for etching. The function of the printing press is essentially the same, which is to apply pressure that is consistent and even. It costs only about RM3,500; an imported printing press would have cost so much more. I think it's good for a miniature product. So there's no reason for young artists to say that they don't have space for a press. A small space is enough to do it.

Clockwise from top:

Rubbing loose pieces of clay onto the engraved parts to reveal the design.

Rolling black offset ink onto the woodblock.

Although there are many common items one may use as a hand-burnishing tool, like seashells or glass, Mansoor chooses the metal spoon to do the job.

Making a stage proof.

(latitudinal section) which is different from woodblock cutting, which uses the opposite (longitudinal section). You can tell how old the tree is by looking at the cross-section of the trunk. Just imagine, a *ciku* tree takes two to three years to grow 1 mm in diameter. It's a waste to throw all these away. For example, the *kemuning* is very expensive. I think, they are selling it by the kilo – one kilo is RM30.

So one of the reasons I switched to engraving was because we do have a surplus of such wood. My friend Fuad used to be a fireman and when he chanced upon such wood that was being thrown away, he would ask for it and bring it back for us. We have managed to collect different types of wood here [at Studio Pena] over the years.

WORKING PROCESS

Describe your typical day. What are some routines that keep you motivated?

My days starts with a bit of workout in the morning, breakfast, and a trip to the market. After that I go to the studio and start with sketching and drawing. In the afternoons I prepare my printing blocks. Every few weeks, I do some printing. In between there's always on-going discussions. Then some reading and a bit of writing. I also enjoy gardening, jogging… and travelling keeps me motivated.

Describe your working process for wood engraving.

For this insect series, I spent almost three months reading up on entomology because I wanted to have a proper documentation of the anatomy for this project. So, I have Fauzi [a fellow artist] send me pictures of these tropical insects. Sometimes we download images from the internet. I also needed to get some professional photographer's work to get blow-ups of the insects because I wanted the textures magnified.

Once I've completed the drawings, I transfer them onto the woodblock. With engraving you cannot make any mistakes. It's different from etching where there is a bigger element of chance involved in the process. For engraving, you must already have a strong mental picture of the design and know how the lines flow in the composition.

Also when you are working only with black ink, your mistakes are magnified. Colour, on the other hand can be deceptive, in a sense that even when you make mistakes, the viewer can be distracted by the colour. But this is not possible with black and white. You will need to start from scratch. So there are no major changes, just minor adjustments.

I digitally inverse the design in Photoshop and then draw it with markers or pencil. Halfway through, you can use a mirror to check the design if you want to see how the print will look like.

How long does it take to engrave one block for the insect series which is about 8 x 6 inches?

One block takes about four hours a day, for about two weeks. It's a nice challenge [laughs]. Usually about 40% into the work, I

Mangsa (Victim) 2013. Once limited edition prints are completed, he 'cancels' the woodblock by signing on it and then makes a proof which bears his reverse signature.

EMELIA ONG

do a stage proof to see how it looks like, and then another one at about 90% completion, because you can't accurately visualise the printed image from the engraving.

Explain your printing process.

Well, I printed this series manually so it does take time. You want to make sure the ink is evenly spread out but you can't be too hard otherwise the paper may tear. So after you ink the woodblock evenly, you can use a spoon to press the ink onto the paper.

This takes about three days to dry. I usually just put a waxy paper on top to protect it before leaving it to dry fully.

Notes

1   English painter and printmaker, the late Sir Stanley William Hayter founded Atelier 17 in Paris (1927), and later in New York City. He published *New Ways of Gravure* in 1949 and became internationally recognised for his innovation in lithography, called viscosity printing.

2   Maktab Perguruan Sultan Idris, formerly, Sultan Idris Teachers College, is currently Universiti Pendidikan Sultan Idris (UPSI) or Sultan Idris Education University.

3   Redza Piyadasa, Tan Teong Eng, Tang Tuck Kan, Sulaiman Esa, Choong Kam Kow.

4   Universiti Teknologi MARA (MARA University of Technology), previously ITM – Institut Teknologi MARA (MARA Institute of Technology).

5   Ciku, Sapodilla (*Manilkara zapota)*, Kemuning (*Murraya paniculata)*, Pokok Asam Jawa, Tamarind tree (*Tamarindus indica*), Penaga Laut, Alexandrian Laurel (*Calophyllum inophyllum)*

6   Traditional Malay dagger characterized by its unique wavy, double-edged damascene blade and pistol-grip handle.

7   Traditional Malay machete.

8   The cross-section obtained by cutting across the grain of the growth rings.

HASNUL J. SAIDON
ENTANGLED BODIES OF ENERGY

Hasnul Saidon is an interdisciplinary media artist who is also an art educator, researcher, writer, editor, curator and museum director. With a strong grounding in drawing and painting, Hasnul is known for using new media during the 1990s, which incorporated video art, electronic art and other time-based media; sometimes including performance as well as participatory and interactive elements.

Although Hasnul may also be rightly called a multimedia artist (as one who works across different media or combines them within a single artwork), the term 'interdisciplinary media' reflects his current efforts to critically incorporate media from disciplines outside of those traditionally considered as art, such as music, film and performance. These pioneering and experimental works examine how new technologies/new media generate different responses and change the way we connect with each other.

His current work, entitled H3RO, is an example of an interdisciplinary media work that encompasses the use of writings, comics, drawings, film, performance, and interactive workshops which are then documented and uploaded to the internet. Based on his blogs about his experiences while growing up with his parents, Hasnul collaborated with the short-film maker, Anderson Ee, to produce a film about his parents. This idea subsequently grew into a larger project that examined the relationship between children and their parents. In these projects he asks,

how do children perceive or relate to their parents? How do their parents make them feel? Touring different towns in Malaysia, he meets school kids, explores these questions with them and helps them to express themselves. Different media elicit different responses from the kids. Each media feeds off the other in order to collectively present a fuller picture of the complex bond between parent and child.

As an art educator who has developed many innovative art curricula for universities like UNIMAS and other art colleges, he aims to help his students realise their own potential in terms of contributing to society through their art practices. Art practice, for him, is a way of developing himself in the service of society. He uses his own art practice and research to drive his pedagogy and curriculum. Thus, both are interrelated; art teaching helps him understand the affective, cognitive and psychomotor domains of learning, whilst the practice of art helps him experience how these domains interact in real life.

Hasnul noted a shift in his practice after taking on the role of curator and museum director of the Tuanku Fauziah Museum and Art Gallery.[1] His art practice began to emphasise interactive processes and moved away from object-centeredness. This focus on audience perception has resulted in works that allow for real exchanges between the artist, the artwork and the audience.

Left: Overseeing the Terengganu style kampung house he is building in Sedim, Kedah, with the help of his daughter Amira who is an assistant architect, Hasnul says, 'As an art educator, I don't believe in learning in traditional classrooms. Universities should get rid of them. As far as lectures are concerned, let's just build an open space with a nice garden and a simple roof. Students should not be going from one box to another. Why do we still use that old concept of a classroom?'

Right: Hasnul loves the fact that the house is just beside the river where kids come to play or fish, and in the afternoon one cools off by taking a dip in the fresh water.

Subsequently, his own doctoral research turned to quantum physics as a way to approach and understand art practice. It helped him go beyond empirically perceived knowledge, to metaphysically perceived higher-level energies. His role as an artist, then, is not as a creator of art objects but of experiences that allow people to tap into higher forms of energy – the spiritual dimensions of experience. Hasnul reiterates that on a quantum level, we are all 'entangled'. However, a society that develops without such transformative artistic experiences tends to produce self-centred individuality, perpetuating an illusion of disconnectedness.

Studies in quantum physics also help him bypass the social and cultural stereotyping that can sometimes be inhibitive when approaching various artistic traditions. Realising the interconnectedness of seemingly opposing artistic traditions or styles, he now works hard to dismantle ideas about art practice that are limited by specific criteria, bounded by media or disciplinary parameters, or those that speak only to a particular audience. As Hasnul declares, everything and everyone is fundamentally connected through energy, at the level of quantum energy. Once we realise that, we can be liberated to practice art without technical or conceptual boundaries. In other words, our preconceptions about what art should be and how it should look would no longer constrain us, allowing for more innovation and originality.

GROWING UP

What were your first exposures to art?

My parents – my mother, especially. She is a mother of nine kids and also a businesswoman. Now, she's around 86. To me, she's a genius. She migrated from a *kampung* (village) to a town in Perak. My father, back then, was a religious teacher, so he received a very small salary. My mother had no choice but to earn extra money. But she's a smart woman. She only attended school up till Standard 6, but she can read Rumi and Jawi[2] She was very good at Mathematics; she can calculate mentally. She has a very strong visual memory, but mostly, she's very creative.

What kinds of jobs did she have?

She was a *tukang jahit* (tailor) and she sold fabrics, batik and so on. She opened a shop and – I'm not sure about this – she might have been the first Malay woman to have a tailor shop in Teluk Intan in the late 1960s. 'Jamaliah Nordin' was a household icon in Teluk Intan, throughout 1960s, 1970s until the 1990s.

My school was not too far from the shop, so I would walk there after school. I grew up with the smell of Singer [brand] sewing machines, the oil, the wooden table where dresses were cut, and the *kapur*, or special chalk for marking fabrics. Everything was done manually then. I remember the fabrics, the cottons, the silks, and the patterns.

She also has green fingers, so I grew up with a lot of greeneries. She loves flowers so much. You could say that she was my first exposure to the arts. I am very blessed. I have wonderful parents.

What about your dad?

My father has passed away. Both of them were total opposites. He would say, 'You need to meditate, get away from the world, go to a mountain,' and my mother would immediately reply, 'If everyone went to the mountain to meditate, who is going to run the country?' So, she would sort of bring him back to reality.

My father was idealistic. To him, our lives was about fulfilling our spiritual potential. He would give the whole family lectures, reciting from old books – we called them *buku kuning*[3] (yellow book) – by Imam Al-Ghazali and other teachers of *tasawwuf*, or Sufism. He emphasised the importance of mystical knowledge.

What does your mother think about what you're doing now, as a professional artist?

Well, because I'm so different from my siblings, she didn't use the same language with me. She always said, '*Aku doakan kamu berguna untuk masyarakat*' (I pray that you will be of good service to society). I said, 'No, no. Don't pray for that. Pray for me to become rich, famous, happy and have a lot of money' [laughs]. But she said, 'No!' So, I want to stop being useful but I can't – because that's my mother's prayer.

Even the school I went to, where my father taught, had this motto, 'Live to Serve' [laughs]. *Hidup Berbakti*. My father really epitomised that 'live to serve' dictum.

LEARNING PROCESS

What are the significant milestones in your learning process?

The first wave are my parents and my teachers. An art teacher who was very important to me was Cikgu Abdul Aziz, from Horley Methodist Primary School. I always went to his house and became close friends with his only son. I was like his *anak angkat* (foster child). He introduced me to oil painting in primary school. He was also painting in his house using the Pointillist technique, with his fingers.

So, I was exposed to painting at an early age, in Standards Four, Five and Six. By Standard Six, I was already painting large sizes, four feet by eight feet. That was in 1978.

A sketch of his mom, Jamaliah Nordin.

HASNUL SAIDON

Above: *Veil of an Artist*, exhibited at the Penang State Art Gallery, 2011, George Town. Video projection/ mapping on mixed media paintings.

HASNUL SAIDON

Left: Detail of one of the panels from Veil of an Artist titled, *Mohon* (Ask) 2010, a mixed media painting.

HASNUL SAIDON

Pictures of his wife and children.

The late Ismail Zain's 1980s Compact Macintosh SE. Malaysian artist Ismail Zain (1930–1991) used this Macintosh to produce his *Digital Collage* (1988) solo exhibition, one of the first to use digital technologies critically as medium and content. Hasnul hopes to restore the data in the computer, which contains the Ismail Zain's notes and groundwork for that exhibition.

The second wave was ITM (Institut Teknologi MARA). At ITM, I was blessed with good teachers at the peak of their performance. They were all different characters who even quarreled amongst each other, but they were very good to me and my colleagues. Choong Kam Kaw, Tan Tuck Kan, Joseph Tan, Ruzaika Omar Basaree, Fauzan Omar, Amrun Omar, Ponirin Amin, Yusof Ghani, Zakaria Awang, Ariffin Ismail, Awang Damit and Ismail Zain was very influential.

Can you tell us about your relationship with Ismail Zain and how he impacted you?

Look, that's his computer and all his CDs. My PhD is based on Ismail Zain's proposition. He said that in order for us to understand tradition better, it should not be approached through history or anthropology but through physics. So, I started my PhD research from that important 1970s statement! I remember reading that many times throughout my life as a student. Then, at one point, I said, 'Why physics?' I'm not good at physics. I almost failed physics in Form Five. But I bravely made myself learn physics and get to know the work of physicists.

Your time in the U.S. was another important milestone?

It was an exciting era for me, the early 1990s. I went to the U.S. from 1989 to 1993. I was supposed to do a MA in painting but I did electronic art instead. I was crazy then, I was bored with painting and didn't learn anything. I was angry at the American professors; all they did was talk, criticise and comment. They also used me as a 'database' for them to teach: via my methods and my techniques. They brought students to see my experiments. I went there to learn, not to have people steal from me. So, I said 'No more painting'.

Then I found Rensselaer Polytechnic,[4] which had the first programme on integrated electronic arts. It was a gamble, I didn't know anything about it and I had to move from Illinois to Troy, New York. That was a very important milestone. I developed serious questions about my early art practices through postmodern and critical theories. Artists like Brenda Miller questioned the role of creative practice in the context of activism and the community. Painting was taken over by the market, part of the economic system… at least that was the mantra then.

When I returned, I couldn't adapt or accept Malaysian art. I even made a cynical work as a response to local contemporary art at that time. But instead, it won an award in *Bakat Muda [Sezaman]*.[5]

How did your time at University Malaysia Sarawak (UNIMAS) shape your art practice?

UNIMAS was a new frontier for me during the 1990s. It was where I practiced what I preached. I met Fauzan [Omar] who was a hardcore painter but very receptive to expanding the practice of fine art. Then there

was Niranjan [Rajah], who gave the team the theoretical foundation and support, there were Wong Hoy Cheong and Liew Kung Yu in the art scene – all very dynamic people. The practice of new media art, electronic media, digital media and the re-questioning and expanding of fine art practice began there. We had the first electronic art show in 1997.

Tell me about your time in Universiti Sains Malaysia (USM).

Academically, it was not as interesting. But an important milestone was being the museum director of the USM Museum and Gallery. I did a lot of audience research. I realised that what was important was not just the artist or the curator but the reaction of the audience to the show. The 'last creative act' actually comes from the audience. I formed the University Museum Network with (Ahmad) Mashadi and Patrick Flores. We did two seminars, one at the University of Philippines, the other at the USM Museum where I expanded on this idea – that the artwork is never finished or settled, or the discourse is never done…

It has really shaped my [current] creative practice, now I always think about who the audience is and what kind of experiences I can offer them. [Similarly], when I have an exhibition, I'm not interested in the creator talking about it. I'd rather get 30 schoolkids and let them talk to me about it. Oh, it's very refreshing! Not pretentious, but very humbling. They don't care if the artists are 'super-artists' or whatever; they don't have that baggage.

When did you stop teaching and why? How has it affected your art practice?

I have stopped teaching for four years to focus on my research. I think I became too tired of teaching for so long. After my academic life, I try not to mix around with clever people [*laughs*]. Instead I realised that I needed to go and see 'actual people'. For example, if you want to know about *masalah sungai* (river issues), don't read about it. Go and meet people who live by the river. Stay with them for a while. Or if you want to teach students about compassion towards animals, ask them to interact with people who take care of animals.

Sometimes people in academia are reading culture rather than experiencing culture. And perhaps I was doing that as well, so I stopped doing it. It's been very liberating.

SPACE AND PLACE

What types of spaces are conducive for your practice?

Well, there should be a space where you can centre yourself. For me, this is extremely important. I think every artist needs to have that. Now, I normally go to my wife's shop.[7] I also have a place in Sedim (Kedah) where I'm building a *kampung* house on a small piece of land just a few yards from the river, as a physical retreat for the family and as an open classroom or lab.

In my house, I have a small garden like a

Hasnul in his ground floor living room-cum-studio space, designed as an open space specially for students and friends to lounge and work in. 'I organise my own work roughly into sections for my editorial works, my publications, newspaper cuttings and videos, then books are sectioned under Film and Music; Islamic Studies; History and Culture; Literature; Education; and Museum collections.'

A space for Hasnul to chill out, jamming with friends, including his numerous beloved cats.

Hasnul conducting a workshop for the project 'H3RO'.

HASNUL SAIDON

Hasnul performing a song and presenting the short film 'H3RO', using a DIY screen and a portable projector and speakers.

HASNUL SAIDON

The audience consists of schoolchildren involved in the project, Hasnul's mother (far left) and wife (middle).

HASNUL SAIDON

typical city dwellers' garden. I have a library. I've got a space where I can sing and perform – singing is a good exercise for breathing – and also a small space to pray and meditate.

How has your idea of a workspace changed since you graduated?

Well, when you first graduate, you want to have a big studio, you need a big space with very nice sunlight. But later on, I realised I don't really subscribe to this idea of having a big studio because I don't like the baggage that comes with that.

We are living in a media-simulated world of impressions and social media. Some artists may feel that you need the persona and impression of having a studio to sustain a name, presence or relevance. You need to have a studio as evidence and testimony of your commitment in that particular market. But when you start to make it a kind of style, to simulate it to make it 'studio-like' or to create an artist's persona, then, I dislike that.

The space should come naturally, because of your working system, your inner self and your inner space, that extends to your studio. Otherwise, the studio becomes – what do

you call it? – *oh, semua orang lain ada studio, saya pun kena ada studio* ('oh, everyone else has a studio, so I must have one too').

CURRENT PRACTICE

Tell me about some of the current projects you've been working on.

For the past four years I have been working on a project called 'H3RO'. On one level, it's about my father. But at another level, it's also about the relationship between children and their parents.

'What is fundamental in our living experience?', 'What do we need the most now?' Those are the questions I ask myself, especially when I was confronted with the death of my father. My father was an extremely strong influence, mentally and emotionally, in my teaching and my spiritual training. He was like Yoda, and my Yoda was gone. It was a wake-up call and a whack on my head.

I then realised that the secret of experiencing life is about *connecting* and *correcting* the connection that has been disconnected. Disconnection is the opposite of compassion, which would be apathy. Apathy is the root of ignorance and hate. I explored that through this project, by looking at how kids perceive their relationship with their parents.

'H3RO' has evolved into a larger project which involves performance but also includes interactive workshops and conversations with kids. Initially, what I did for 'H3RO' was basically two short films. I did it together with my friend, Anderson Ee, a short-film maker. Later, I wrote and performed three original songs with my daughter,[7] and also presented oral stories through PowerPoint slides. I had a very small projector unit and we identified who our audiences would be and went on a tour.

When I performed with my daughter at Hin Bus Depot, my friend asked, 'So, you're not doing art anymore?' I *am* doing art, I'm singing, I'm singing in public. [I told my daughter] we are changing the visual energy of sound. There is an aural energy of George Town, created by traffic. So, when we sing, we are enriching the aural energy of George Town on the streets, not just in the gallery.

Where have you performed so far?

I have brought 'H3RO' to eight or nine places already. It premiered in a *dusun* (orchard) in Balik Pulau,[8] and Dusun Pak Sarip at Gertak Sanggul.[9] And then I brought it to UMS (Universiti Malaysia Sabah), UNIMAS, Seri Iskandar,[10] Perak, and Pulau Dayang Bunting in Langkawi. I've even brought it to the National Art Gallery (Kuala Lumpur). It's a mobile presentation.

Different places have different sorts of energy. When I go to the *dusun*, the *dusun* energy is awesome. Like Pulau Dayang Bunting[11] (Langkawi), which is my friend's place by the sea, under the stars – very interesting energy.

This is a commissioned project?

Initially, it was self-funded for about one and a half years. After KLB (Kuala Lumpur: Belas) became [KL] Biennale,[12] this became part of an outreach project by the National Art Gallery to get different sections of the community to engage with the concept of *Gema Belas* which means Echo of Compassion. They funded me for one year.

Hasnul illustrates his father taking him for rides on a kapcai (motorcycle) and other scenes of daily life growing up in a big family. These form an extensive compilation of DIY comics and drawings.

HASNUL SAIDON

MATERIALS AND TOOLS

Tell me how you select materials. What goes into the decision-making process?

Well, I'm not a material-specific practitioner. But neither do I believe that one can just use anything as material or have a nebulous idea of material. I don't believe in 'anything goes', or in saying, 'Oh, everything is experimental'. At one point, yes – by not limiting your materials. But you do have to focus on something you want to explore.

I have a clear idea of what I'm trying to accomplish, and the questions I'm trying to ask, then I say, 'What's the best way to make the audience think about this, or to generate this experience?' and 'What's the best medium to get an honest response?'

The audience cannot relate to facts. They're not interested in clever arguments or theory. You can theorize something by yourself but when you engage the public, they're not interested. They don't care about the artists or what concept they're using. But you can reach them through their hearts. And to do that, you need stories. Not concepts but narratives.

Can you describe some differences between painting and video as a medium? Or between video and live performance?

When I use narratives and present them in my video, or sing, I look into their eyes, and I see a different energy than those who look at my painting. I cannot describe it. For 'H3RO', I looked at the kids looking at the screen. I feel a different 'high' looking them, compared to looking at audiences viewing my work at the gallery. Now, why is that? I am not sure. It's a different kind of energy.

Hasnul and his daughter Ainina performing at Hin Bus Depot.

AININA HASNUL

Hasnul and his wife, the batik artist Rozana Mohamed, at the shop.

SN KHOO

For me, it's a journey that is very humbling and I'm very thankful that I use this method. If I just screen my video and show it amongst 'art people', or just make a visual artwork and exhibit or sell it, my friends may say good things, collectors will buy and I'll get some money but I don't think I'll get this experience. So, I'm very thankful that I changed the methods and approaches of my creative practice because I cannot pay for this.

Can you talk about the style that you chose for this film?

I wanted it to be technically straightforward, so there are no effects, no tweaking or editing in terms of colour or grain, *et cetera*. We used either black-and-white or colour to differentiate time periods. I did not want it to be overly romanticised, but we were basically re-staging the past so we couldn't do hardcore realism either [laughs].

I also don't believe in melodrama, where characters have to cry to make audiences cry. Or where you have to be angry for your ideas to be angry. Instead, you can use small triggers that your audience can respond to. When you do that, they will create their own performance through your work, which creates an interesting field of energy. That's awesome. And that energy interacts with the energy of the place and of your work.

WORKING PROCESS

Can you describe your typical day?

I wake up, water the plants, feed my cat, clean his space, get all the bad energy and trash out of the house. Sometimes I go jogging at the park. Then I say prayers to my late father, all my gurus, teachers and all who have contributed to me. Before I step out of the house, I always say that today is awesome. Even if anything is bad, there must be something good hiding behind it. I always say so.

How much does social media shape your work?

I don't like social media but I use it, because this is the world we are living in. We need to ask ourselves what kinds of messages we want to spread. A lot of people use it to gossip, but we need to use it in more positive ways. I use them to document my working process. My essays and documentation are all on Facebook and my blog. I use Behance for my portfolio.[13]

Can you describe your working process for 'H3RO'? How did it start and what was involved in the decision-making processes?

When I did 'H3RO', my father was still alive. My friend, Anderson, read my blog and said, 'Hasnul, I've read most of your writings. In all your writings, you try to be clever. But in this one, you are being truthful to yourself.' I wasn't so serious about that blog, but he said, 'I want to make a film about it. I want to see your father.' So, we did the first one while my father was still alive.

He passed away three months later. I couldn't watch the first film for a year. After that, I told Anderson, 'We need to give a good ending to the first film.' Subsequently, we did the second film, 'H3RO Epilogue'.

Can you describe the working roles between you and Anderson for this project?

I worked on the storyline and the script, and he translated it into shots. We'd go to the *mamak* [14] and look over the storyboards. He handled the difficult job of editing – he had to change it over fifty times! Our film was only five minutes each. The shorter the film, the harder it is to edit.

Did you have a time frame in mind when you started this project?

Partly, yes. You don't have to force it, you can let it flow. But it's important to have a clear intention from the beginning. For example, now I have the materials but I haven't decided what to do with that. I don't know whether I should come up with a show, a book or a Facebook page. Maybe I'll create an interactive or DIY book. So, half the book will be filled by the reader, half from me. Everybody will buy the same book but will end up having a different book.

Can you recall what made you focus specifically on the relationship between kids and their parents?

One way to explore the basic idea of connection is to go back to your root of being – from which your [sense of] connection came – in your father and mother. That made the most sense to me. That has been the thematic framework that I use again and again for the past three or four years since I did 'H3RO'. Also, those ideas on connection were related to my research [15] on quantum physics and art for my PhD.

How did your research on quantum physics impact your approaches to art practice?

A lot of what I learned was not just an academic exercise as I was able to apply it in my projects. For example, we need to approach the mind in a more holistic way.

Quantum physics reveals that our minds have different stages of vibrations. In our lower consciousness, the mind is centered on the idea of separateness. However, when we engage in a higher vibrational level, our illusive sense of separateness dissolves. Our self-centeredness dissolves. I'm not talking here about becoming a monk [laughs]. I'm talking about opening pathways that allow love and compassion to take place.

Notes

1 The Muzium & Galeri Tuanku Fauziah (MGTF) at the Universiti Sains Malaysia (USM), Penang, was initiated after the establishment of the School of Humanities and the introduction of the Fine Art Programme in 1971 and 1972 respectively. USM was the first public university in Malaysia to pioneer the offering of Fine Arts as a discipline at a higher education level.

2 Rumi is the Malay term referring to the Latin alphabet used in writing Romanised Malay script. Jawi is the Malay term referring to the Arabic alphabet used in spelling out Malay words.

3 Literature used for Islamic education is known as *Kitab Kuning* (Yellow Religious Book) because it was conventionally printed on yellow coloured paper.

4 The Department of Arts at Rensselaer Polytechnic in Troy, New York championed the use of electronic media and a multidisciplinary approach to produce art during the 1970s.

5 Bakat Muda Sezaman (Young Contemporaries) began in 1974 as an initiative by the Balai Seni Lukis Negara (National Art Gallery), Malaysia, to support emerging Malaysian artists. Hasnul's work entitled *Mirror, Mirror on the Wall* won a minor award in 1994.

6 Hasnul's wife, Rozana Mohamed, is an artist who works primarily with textiles. She is also the owner of 'Rozana's Batik', a shop on Lebuh Acheh, George Town, which sells batik fabrics and batik art, and conducts workshops for foreign tourists.

7 Hasnul has three daughters: Ainina who performs his songs with him, Adeela who assists with photo documentation, and Amira an assistant architect helping with the construction of his house in Sedim.

8 Balik Pulau in the southwestern district of Penang island is known for its durians, paddy fields and newly emerging cultural attractions.

9 Gertak Sanggul is a fishing village and agricultural town on the southwestern coast of Penang Island.

10 Seri Iskandar is a satellite town comprising a university township in central Perak.

11 The second largest island south of Langkawi, Pulau Dayang Bunting (Pregnant Maiden Island) is known for its fresh water lake.

12 Hasnul was part of the planning committee in the National Art Gallery for an exhibition themed *Belas* (Beloved). This idea was partly adapted for the first ever Kuala Lumpur Biennale in Malaysia, with the theme *Alami Belas* (Be Loved), held November 2017–March 2018.

13 Blog, Hasnul J Saidon@Kebun Jiwa Halus; Facebook, GemaBelas2017; Behance, Hasnul J Saidon.

14 Local South Indian Muslim cafés, traditionally set up as open-air eateries by the roadside.

15 On-going thesis titled, 'Re-approaching Islamic Visual Tradition through the Language of Quantum Physics.'

GAN CHIN LEE
THE ART OF BALANCE

Gan Chin Lee is an oil painter who paints the human figure in its contemporary everyday context. He is also an art educator at The One Academy where he first trained as an illustrator. Today he is recognised as a contemporary realist, known for his thought-provoking depictions of Malaysian urban life. His painting approaches were developed from his classical training in Beijing, which was gradually refined to reflect his personal temperament as well as his outlook towards subject matter.

Gan studied fine art at the Central Academy of Fine Arts where he explored various approaches and techniques towards painting: from Classicism, to Neo-Classicism to Romanticism, to Impressionism. He has since developed his own style of painting which combines his fascination for the figurative with more technical considerations for the different methods of layering paint.

In his practice, he strives to produce what he terms Avant-Garde Realism; in other words, a fresh take on Realism. Realism was an art movement during the mid-19th century, where artists sought to represent their subject matter more 'truthfully' and without romantic stylisations. The 'real' replaced the 'ideal' as subject matter. Since then, various approaches to Realism in art have reflected the changing ideas about what constitutes the 'truth' or the 'real'. Realism began to reflect the complexities involved in redefining the 'real' through visual, physical, psychological or spiritual experiences. Today, contemporary artists who worked within a realist mode, such as Gan, no longer subscribe to easy definitions of what the 'real' is.

Gan's practice becomes a way of making sense of his own experiences living in Malaysia. His titles reflect a range of themes such as hybridity, urban society, migration, and diaspora. These themes capture our collective urban concerns and how we think about ourselves in relation to society. He notes that contemporary life has been marked by migration.

The phenomenon of migration has subsequently engendered a sense of displacement, not only for the immigrant but also for the locally-born. Gan skilfully captures these tensions in the expression and composition of his figures. His works enunciate the balance involved in maintaining our individual identities as they are subsumed within collective identities. He is also insistent that a unique method of paint application be produced to reflect such contemporary anxieties.

Traditional methods can no longer translate the new urges and struggles of the present. They need to be adapted, reworked and transformed. Gan has been honing his techniques for the past ten years in order to reflect the negotiations between the traditional and the contemporary, the urban and the rural, the self and the other. His approach to life as well as to art seems

I'm in Mamak Stall. 2008.
Oil on linen.
GAN CHIN LEE

Kedai Kopi Sungai Jarom,
2011. Oil on Linen.

'When I first started painting, what got me fascinated in the beginning, was the beauty of layering in oil painting – the nuanced colour changes that you get with the layering method, that transparent quality of paint. I like that kind of beauty.'

to centre on this consistent effort to find a middle ground, in order to achieve that balance.

Finally, his contemplations about contemporary realism are essentially his attempts to understand opposing ways of thinking among different communities, whether of different ages, cultures or environments. He concludes that ultimately, we need to find ways of living together peacefully without conflict or violence. Thus the artist speaks critically through his practice and becomes the voice of moderation.

GROWING UP

Can you recall your earliest exposures to art?

I loved comics a lot… Hong Kong comics, Japanese comics like 'Dragon Ball'. Initially I thought I would end up as a comic artist.

When I went to The One Academy, I wanted to be a comic artist and I studied Illustration for that purpose. After graduation I worked for two years as a comic artist but it was very different from what I had imagined.

How is it different?

If you want to create a successful comic strip, it is not about your drawing skills. It is about how you tell a story. The script is very important, and the storyboarding as well, but I found that I was not interested in that. I realised that I enjoyed producing single paintings more than creating storyboards.

When I was small, I was also quite addicted to Chinese woodcut prints and paper cuttings, like those we often see during Chinese New Year, for example, a child holding a fish, and so forth. These things sometimes come back to me in my practice.

In my current practice I try to absorb

the formality of *ukiyo-e*[1] and Chinese traditional woodcut prints. I try to combine that kind of flat beauty into my traditional style of figurative paintings. I want to create something fresh, by inventing some kind of so-called Avant-Garde Realism.

LEARNING PROCESS

What was it like to switch from commercial illustration to fine art?

In the commercial line, I got to step 'out of the image' and think about pleasing the client or target audience. But fine arts is about the artist's ego and you've got to put your own observations into the painting. It is not about an acceptance of the audience. Instead, you've got to lead the audience to think, and you've got to think of pushing the boundaries of the visual language in contemporary trends. For me, it's a lot harder.

Can you recall the time when you were studying Illustration at The One Academy, how has that been beneficial to your practice now?

Somehow it strengthened my foundational skills and my self-organising attitude. Like I couldn't really work from day until night constantly, so they taught me to be alert [to stay focussed], work ethics, self-discipline.

During that time, I also learned some computer skills. That's why I now use Photoshop, Illustrator, these kinds of software quite effectively. So, in my final stages, I will use these softwares to speed up the progress.

It also helped me to not shy away from modern technology and software. I think classical approaches in painting works better when combined with more advanced technology.

You went to the Central Academy of Fine Arts in Beijing to study painting. Can you describe that experience?

There was so much culture shock. I thought I would do quite well but the comments from the professor were not so encouraging. Gradually, I refined my techniques in a few years. That's why it's important to learn from art history. When I look at how different artists interpret the way they are seeing, I correct my old habits from them.

What made you choose that Academy?

The system in Beijing Academy is different. We've got to take an exam to be accepted. First, for Art History, then for Drawing, then for Painting. They give you a test, then randomly give you a title. You've got to react to the title on the spot. They also categorise their studios into four studios: So I'm in the first studio which focused on paintings from the art periods of Classicism until Impressionism. The second studio is more focused on combining Expressionism with Chinese aesthetics. The third studio would be more focused on contemporary issues. Then the fourth studio is really focused on materials and methods.

What were some of the prevailing painting approaches taught whilst you were studying at the Academy?

Actually, ten years ago, figuration was still the mainstream genre within the Beijing art circles, but now it's falling out of trend. But China is huge and there are many different circles. Guangzhou is very different in their ideology – very experimental and conceptual. But in Beijing, a lot of artists still do propaganda-type paintings that portray the beauty of the labourer... those types of subject matter.

How did the Academy approach painting?

In the 1970s, they were very much into Russian realistic paintings. They sent people to Russia to study the methodology – how to start learning about the figure from the skeletal structure and musculature. Then, I think after the 1990s, there was a big change. A lot of people graduated from Europe. More avant-garde thoughts developed. Many went to Europe to study the development of Realism, not Social Realism, but the contemporary development of Realism.

I remember that we observed a lot of different body types for models. From youngsters to adults, to old people. They taught me not to limit yourself to just appreciate one or two types of anatomy while I was studying. Both skinny people and fat people have got their own beauty, it depends on how you understand the inner relation to structure, those sorts of things. Then after you graduate, you can decide what kind of body type you are more interested in.

Working on a triptych, his current work captures various aspects of migration, and the transitions people go through when moving from the village to an urban environment.

Works in progress: Gan's painting stands on the easel, while Jennifer's leans against the wall in one the rooms upstairs, which has also been converted into a studio.

What about Abstraction? Were they outwardly against it?

In their opinion, no matter how good you are [in abstraction], you are still [copying] European artists, you wouldn't be more avant-garde than them. Then, they say if you want to work in abstraction, choose Chinese ink painting, which is more 'true'.

Who was your teacher?

Hu Jian Cheng. He was a classical painter. They define themselves as Neoclassical painters, interested in the concept or the meaning of contemporary realism.

I am always interested in drawing the figure, anatomical subjects, so I appreciate the historical knowledge I gained from the first studio. Although in the future, I might not continue in that kind of approach [taught in that studio]; but I wanted to start from there.

SPACE AND PLACE

What brings you to this current space?

I bought this house because it's close to my hometown in Jenjarom, so I can go back to visit my parents very often. It's just about 20 minutes away. It is also in between my hometown and working area in Sunway. I have a car, so this location is not a problem for me. I like this sort of peaceful and quiet environment, also to have a better excuse to skip all those activities in town.

How often do you teach?

Two times a week, so the rest of the time I spend in my studio.

This is my first studio. I'm thinking of moving to another area because currently, this place is obviously too small for both of us (me and my wife Jennifer,[2] who is also an artist). We think it's better to separate the working area from the residence.

How does sharing a space with your spouse affect your working style or working process?

Sometimes I run out of this studio to go to the coffee shop, so that I can really focus on my writings or thoughts. And sometimes when I do research, I would rather she [my wife] not join me. We try not to influence each other too much.

While working I don't allow her to step into my area. I don't allow her to throw her opinion about too directly before I ask. So, I set the rules, if I don't ask you, don't simply give any feedback. But when I pass through the living room, I will surely see her work and, sometimes, she will stop me to ask for my opinion of her current work.

CURRENT PRACTICE

Can you talk about your current interest in the migration topic?

I think this interest stems from my cultural identity as a third generation Chinese immigrant. I think, because we live in Malaysia, we [my family] couldn't really relate to the 5,000 years of art and cultural development in China.

When I started this series, I did research on migrants all over the world. Migrants from

other countries such as the Filipinos in Hong Kong, the Africans in the U.S., the Irish in the U.K. …and there were a lot of similarities in their experiences. I did that to get a sense of the experience of migration, but essentially, my work still centres on what is happening locally. And it's not so much about what is happening cross country [transnationally], but what is happening when you move from the village to the city.

I came from a Chinese New Village,[3] and when I came to the city, there was this culture shock. The infrastructure and the way society lived. It was in total conflict.

When I was researching this topic, I got a chance to talk to the people who still live in the New Villages today. Their ideologies are so different. It's important that we learn to understand each other and be able to communicate. How do we gain acceptance and tolerance for each other? How do I get this balance? This is one of the hardest things to learn.

Do you try to maintain a connection to life in the village?

Definitely. That is why I chose Shah Alam. Because it is a place that is closer to nature. However, what I like about modern life is the convenience it brings. There are many things we do today that are a lot easier. So, we need to find that balance between modern life and maintaining our relationship to nature.

It is difficult, but it is our responsibility to continue to fight. As an artist, I want to create something inspiring from this struggle, to urge people to continue thinking about this.

MATERIALS AND TOOLS

What kind of linen do you use and do you prime the linen yourself?

Currently I'm using Korean linen. It has a richer texture which dominates the final visual outcome. I also use some China imported linen, which is cheaper. Of course, some suppliers sell good quality linen from the U.S. or European countries, but those are a lot more expensive.

Now I just buy primed linen which is acceptable. But I do quite enjoy the process of priming the linen myself, because I can decide how bold it is and try out more possibilities.

What brands of oil paints do you use and where do you source them?

I use Winsor & Newton and Old Holland. I got my first Old Holland oils from France the very first time when I visited. After that, I got addicted to the quality of the oil. At that time, KL suppliers didn't sell any Old Holland colours. The nearest place was Singapore, so I had to travel there. Then, two years ago, we persuaded Ricky, the owner of Premier Art in Publika, to start bringing in this brand.

Gan painting in his studio which is actually a renovated extension off the back of his house, transforming what used to be the backyard into a quiet, well-lit work space.

Clockwise, from top left:

A portable French wooden travel easel used for *plein-air* painting during his schooldays.

Custom-made by his brother for less than RM300, this stainless steel trolley accommodates all his paint tubes, palette and brushes.

Half-used tubes of Old Holland oils, well-known for its brilliance and permanence in colour quality. Gan's preferred brand, Old Holland's trademark is the colour strip above the label which is not printed but painted with the actual colour straight from the tube for accuracy.

Neatly stacked new tubes of oils and bottles of solvents and mediums which include thickened linseed oil, refined linseed oil, gloss varnish, liquin original medium and paper sealers.

Do you have any special preferences for the solvents you use?

I buy odourless turpentine because I have a sinus problem and I can't bear that kind of smell. I use mostly linseed oil. I also use solvents as a better quality turpentine and then liquin, the transparent gel which smoothens the colours. Basically, these are the most common mediums that I use. Since I chose oil, I know it is quite bad for health so I try to make my studio as open as possible. Some particular oil colours can be bad. Like Cadmium Yellow and Zinc White.

Do you use something other than the basic traditional art materials to paint?

I'm in transition between the old and the new. In the beginning, I tried using the computer to do digital paintings for about 2 to 3 years, but I didn't like it. It was distracting and I developed neck and spine problems from sitting in front of the computer. I also don't like that kind of feeling, adjusting brush strokes on the screen and having the same physical momentum. I don't like that kind of 'fake' feel. So now I only use it to supplement my painting and combine it with traditional approaches.

WORKING PROCESS

Normally the procedure of my painting process is separated into a few stages. The first stage is outdoor research. I will go out every day and research the things I'm interested in.

Line sketch, camera, record, documentation, interview. When I enter the production stage I will wake up before 7 a.m. or so, and after breakfast and all sort of things, I will start to work on it – at least 10 hours per day or longer than that. I will not step outside anymore. Even if there are activities in town I will still focus on my work. During this period, it is very hard to step out of my paintings and still talk normally to other people – I will be thinking of the paintings all the time.

So, after the production stage, there will be another stage; that is, working with the gallery, like photo shooting, inviting the writer to write on the works, *et cetera*.

I think public holidays mean nothing to me right now. Every week I spend two days – but most of the time more than two days – at the Academy (teaching). So I try to work as much as I can for the rest of the days.

How long do you work on a painting?

It depends on the size and, since I am working on a few pieces together at the same time, [it is hard to tell]. But, on average, one painting per month. So in a year, I would only produce 10 to 12 pieces of paintings.

Right now, I'm figuring out a new painting style. So I'm looking for a new visual language which combines the *alla prima*[4] painting style with *chiaroscuro*[5] painting style. So, this is faster compared to a typical *chiaroscuro* painting [process].

How do you maintain the spontaneity in your figure drawings when you work with photographs?

My previous learning process is very important. When I was in Beijing, I was totally drawing from 'life' [models]. In those few years, I established my own methodology. I don't blindly follow the reference. I get whatever I want from the photo, and then combine that with my own drawing habits and my sense of aesthetics. I do my own sketches. It helps me to maintain 'originality'. I don't rely on the projector but I use a very traditional construction method. I use proper gridlines and enlarge images from my sketches according to the gridlines.

How do you decide when the work is complete? Does that depend more on the concept or on the style of painting?

It's very difficult to say. Every piece is different. When I think that I have created enough visual interest, I leave it. It could still be very raw but it is complete.

For example, when I look at a classical painting… I feel like it is too refined. I prefer something more spontaneous. I get inspiration from Velázquez[6], a Spanish painter who has a kind of raw touch and raw brush work. While layering, I found that certain textures looked nice when I decide not to overpaint it. I want to reserve that kind of natural texture or brushwork and maintain that spontaneity.

When you use photographs as references, does that in anyway affect the way you compose?

I compose it mentally first and then use the photos as my supporting materials. But I need to compromise. If I have the budget, I could hire people to sit for me and that would be the best way. But in Malaysia it's very hard to achieve that because the selling price of artworks cannot compare to those in Taiwan or China. There, being able to sell for a higher price means that [those artists] can imagine more ways to help enhance their execution. But the price of artworks in Malaysia would not compensate for these types of practices, which can be costly. So I have to choose [my method] and I have to get used to it. But I have sorted it out and solved this problem by taking photographs.

How does teaching affect your work?

It's good and bad. Teaching occupies some of my personal time and, when I am painting, I get distracted by the things I need to do as a teacher. However, the good thing is that I always get some unexpected inspiration from my students. It's something I never thought about. And when I do preparation for lectures, I also learn during this process.

Crit session[7]: Gan with his students from The One Academy.

GAN CHIN LEE

Notes

1   Ukiyo-e is a Japanese term meaning 'pictures of the floating world', referring to the distinct Japanese woodblock print art forms popularised during the Edo period (17th–19th centuries) in Japan.

2   Gan's wife, Jennifer Liu Hsin Ying is a Taiwanese artist who is now based in Malaysia.

3   During the 1950s, the British colonial government created over 400 new settlements as a counter-measure against presumed communist anti-colonial guerrilla forces. Over one million people were forced out of their homes and resettled into these 'New Villages', which were fenced and guarded to prevent communist influence and coercion. Today, the remaining inhabitants of these New Villages consist of a marginalised ageing population who lack access to wider community support.

4   *Alla prima* is an Italian term for 'first attempt', also known as 'wet-on-wet', a technique for oil painting that requires the fast application of new paint on a freshly painted previous layer, while it is still wet.

5   *Chiaroscuro* is an Italian term for 'light-dark', a technique of contrasting the effects of light and shadow to depict three-dimensional form and volume.

6   Diego Rodríguez de Silva y Velázquez (1599–1660) was the leading Spanish Baroque painter in the court of King Philip IV and one of the most significant artists of the Spanish Golden Age.

7   The 'crit' or critique session is an evaluative exercise during which the student presents his or her work. The critique group consisting of faculty and students will provide the student with feedback, constructive questions, advice, and frank comments.

JENNIFER LIU HSIN YING
LIBERATED BODIES

As a young and emerging artist in the Malaysian art scene, Jennifer Liu's works are simultaneously playful, provocative and mature. Working in both two-dimensional forms like drawing and painting, as well as video and performance art, Jennifer appreciates the different processes and elements involved in multimedia works. She says, each type of media offers unique ways of exploring the world—this provides a necessary diversity for the artist, presenting alternative paths towards the same destination.

Originating from Taiwan, Jennifer was educated in a rigorous school system that recognised the importance of learning the arts as part of the formal school curriculum. She was thus trained in the study of art as a serious subject since the age of 10. This traditional training gave her a strong grounding in the basic technical skills of drawing and painting, and nurtured an approach of asking questions through art which she continues to practice today. She muses that by the time she was in college, art had become a natural way for her to express herself and answer life's questions.

An aspect of life that continually piques her curiosity is the nature of human desire and motivation. Why do we do the things we do? What makes us do it? Why do we act in certain ways? These are some of the questions that she considers through artistic exploration. She uses varied media depending on the type of elements she would like to express. Each medium operates within differing contexts and engages the audience differently.

She sees charcoal and pastels, for instance, as mediums that help her to express herself instinctively. Markers or acrylic paints are useful for instantaneous mark making and spontaneous action. At other times, videography is used when she considers questions about sexuality, desire and womanhood. It is an ideal format that helps her think about representations of the body as a woman and how the body has been sexualised by the media. Since the 1960s, artists have begun using the body as a point of departure to discuss racial, cultural, gendered and sexualised identities. Through video and performance art, Jennifer says, she employs the body to negotiate 'her own journey as a woman'.

In some of her works, her body is used as a political medium of performance to resist stereotypical notions of what a woman represents. In a work called *Girls Parade* (2017), Jennifer teams up with her friend and co-artist for a performance piece, where they dress up as female escorts who go about doing normal activities on the street. They comment on the representation of women in the media, proliferated particularly by Disney movies. Women, they state, have been pictured as naïve princesses or strong independent heroines in Disney narratives. By creating a sense of discomfort, they draw the public into a discussion about how women's roles in society have been essentialised.

Jennifer also privileges performance art for its ability to connect directly with different audiences. One of the integral characteristics

Heart, Flesh Mind. 2014.
Mixed Media.
JENNIFER LIU

of performance art is its interactivity with the public. The fact that it is performed live, gives it a sense of suspense. She has used performance art to playfully explore normative behaviours in society, and to question the so-called rules that govern our public behaviour.

She uses performance to interrupt daily routines and question various socially-performed actions. Since performance art does not operate by a set of rules, Jennifer says, this liberates the artist from having to conform to social expectations. Ultimately, this is what she loves about art – that it grants her the license to express herself honestly and break social conventions that limit the genuine expressions of ourselves and others.

GROWING UP

Can you tell me about your first exposure to art?

When I was 4 or 5 years old, I loved drawing and I would invite my friends to come over to my house so that we could all draw together. We would pile up the pillows so we could draw on the ceiling.

My parents were okay with it because they saw that it made me happy and kept me happy. So, my friends loved coming over! My father worked in a company in marketing, while my mom was a travel agent.

Can you think about how your interest in art developed?

When I was about 10, I was selected in my class to focus on art. A few students were selected after undergoing a test, to focus on either art or music. These students would have extra art classes on Mondays and Thursdays for the whole afternoon, on top of the usual classes. This [routine] continued throughout High School.[1] It was quite difficult, because we had to keep up with the usual schedule but also put in extra effort in these art classes.

What was your favourite subject matter as a child?

Mostly, what I see every day. I love animals and nature, the river, the mountains, my family, my dog... it was pretty straightforward, as these were things I thought beautiful.

Then, I remember my friend highlighting to me that if I were only to draw the beautiful side of life, I cannot develop my art in a deeper way. So, I have to really know myself and look at things truthfully. I became more critical in my art and began questioning more. Then, my art did not look as bright or as sweet or pure as it used to, because I wanted to express the changes that I felt while growing up. It became more complicated, less naïve, more emotionally expressive. My art today often begins with questions about things I want to find out. I use art to help me find the answers.

LEARNING PROCESS

During high school, I acquired the basic skills of making art, like sketching, drawing and using watercolours. The teaching approach was very traditional. However, in my second year of high school, one of the teachers started to do more creative work with us. He asked us to think of 100 questions that we need to ask ourselves. Then we created 100 works in response to those questions. That was how I started to learn to ask questions and use that as an approach in my practice.

My third year was more focused on improving my techniques to prepare my portfolio for entrance into university (Taipei National University of the Arts),[2] where I had to submit three pieces of works.

When I entered university, my work expanded in terms of the size. My paintings became bigger and bigger. I also started using pastels. I also realised I could use my body to produce art.

I was exposed to different forms of contemporary art such as performance art and video art for the first time. And I also started to be interested in the state of space, and tried to understand space in different ways. From that time onwards, my boundaries in art continued to expand.

You went to The Arts Students League of New York for your studies. How did that experience affect your art practice?

I had certain expectations about going to New York because it was the first time I had gone to a Western country. I suppose I thought they were more advanced. But the institute was very traditional. When they analysed a painting, I was shocked to find out that it was very similar to how we did it in Taiwan!

Why did you choose that place?

Many famous artists learnt from them and it was also quite cheap.

I like the energy of New York. It was in New York that I started drawing on the streets with charcoal. But I was there for only two months, then I left to travel on my own to the west coast; California, Las Vegas, Grand Canyon, Niagara Falls. …I produced sketches during this time.

Through these experiences my thinking as a person remained the same… but the image in my mind has changed… my perceptual experience was broadened, my colour palette changed. Also, I started thinking more about home. So my journey out of Taiwan makes me contemplate the concept of home. I went back for one more year to finish my degree.

Overall, my university experience widened my scope and considerations about art.

CURRENT PRACTICE

Tell me about the project you just completed during your residency in Shanghai.

For this residency [in June 2017], my partner/collaborator[3] and I had chanced upon this village and the people who live there. They were known to live by certain traditional moral or family precepts (家訓 *jiā xùn*) passed down by their ancestors. We found it really interesting to learn that each family in this town had a written set of 'family precepts' from which to adhere to. These precepts were hung on the walls

Ado ra ble. Girls Parade Show, Taiwan, 2017. (Performance) Jennifer (right) and Xu perform a series of everyday activities dressed as call-girls (social escorts) to bring attention to the gender stereotyping of women. They challenged the community around them to rethink what constitutes female identity.
JENNIFER LIU

Work in progress, Shanghai. Jennifer enjoys performance that questions conventional rules of behavior. The performance seeks to interrupt the hustle and bustle of daily routines in the city.
JENNIFER LIU

Family Precepts Aerobics of Xian Qiao village, China. 2017. Still frame of the performance. On right: Jennifer Liu and Xu Yi Ting performing the exercise with one of the villagers.

JENNIFER LIU

of their houses. So we decided to do a performance based on this.

The performance was designed as a form of aerobic exercise with music. We also had a script which were basically reiterations of the rules. So, as the exercise is being performed, we would recite these rules. This exercise was accompanied by the person living in that particular house. The performance was then recorded with subtitles added.

You planned this work as a performance piece before you went to China?

Well, yes, because we had to give a rough proposal of our ideas for the residency. But we made changes to the project once we met the townsfolk. For example, we realised that the so-called traditional precepts were actually rules provided by the government. So, we produced the videos to highlight that contradiction.

Installation as part of Family Precepts Aerobics of Xian Qiao Village, China.

JENNIFER LIU

So, an important part of your practice is to allow your interaction with the subject matter to change the way you present the work?

Yes, for example, when we arrived, we met an old man in the village who had been living alone. When we saw his house, we were struck by the fact that he had reserved a portion of his house [and kept it] unoccupied for his son, even though his son had not visited for a long time. There was a lot of emptiness in that house and we felt that. So we try to capture that energy in the last portion of the work, where we decided to do an installation.

At first we were just going to play the video on TV, but after visiting him, we decided to project the image of the abandoned house on the wall. And the TV screening the video [was placed] facing the wall instead of an audience because we wanted to relate the emptiness or loneliness that we found in that place. It was also significant because, in actuality, after we made the video, there was no audience for it.

SPACE AND PLACE

How does being in a different environment like this (Malaysia) affect your art?

Malaysia is multi-ethnic and that is something different for me. But there is no difference living in Malaysia or Taiwan because it's not the change of environment that impacts me.

Is there a difference when you are working outside of your studio?

Once I was at Sunway Pyramid and I was drawing on my body while recording myself on video. Someone walked up to me and asked me not to do it in front of the shops. So I walked away from the shops a little bit and continued. Again, he walked up to me and asked me to move out of the shopping area. So I had to move.

In my experience, people in Taiwan tend to be more nervous than in China. When I was in China (Shanghai) people don't seem to care that much, or they may come up and ask me if I'm making a movie and they would be fine with it and leave me alone. But in Taiwan they seem to be more self-conscious.

But so far, the environment is not a factor when it comes to my work. Like I said, it's more of the change of lifestyle that has made a difference. Like being married is a bigger influence for me… because it changes my daily experience.

What is it like sharing the same space as your husband?

We are very different. I am messy, and he is more tidy [laughs]. His work is more structured but I usually go with what inspires me at the moment …I am more spontaneous. So, we maintain separate work spaces. I was actually working upstairs in one of the rooms but I felt confined because it was a smaller space – after a while I decided to just bring my work down to the living room so that I am free to walk around my work.

MATERIALS AND TOOLS

Do you favour using any particular type of media?

In terms of art materials, I do like using charcoal because to me charcoal is pure and simple. I can just crush it with my hand. It is just like the soil or the earth.

I'm not selective about different brands of art materials. But I do buy my canvas from Taiwan because it's cheaper.

What do you like about performance art and about using your body to express your ideas?

The world outside is like a playground to me. But we are expected to live by certain norms and behaviours. With performance art, you can cross the line and do things you normally can't.

I use it as an opportunity to experiment, for example, in my performance called *We Are Here* (2014), I tried to create various emotions and experiences in a span of five days. Working with a co-artist: on the first day, we screamed;

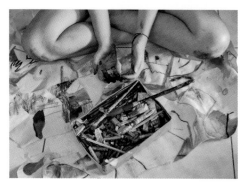

Jennifer and husband, Gan Chin Lee sharing a conversation about how as a couple, they need their own separate space to work in, so that there is time spent completely alone with their own works. Gan says, 'I think it's important not to influence each other when you're in the middle of the work. But interestingly, my friends tell me my palette has become more colourful after I met her.'

Jennifer with her box of loose crayons, pastels, brushes, markers from which she works. She is not particular about her art materials, she says, 'I use whatever I find in the art shops or in the stationery shop.'

on the second, we spoke our mind; on the third, we leaned on the wall; on the fourth, we cried; and on the fifth, we laughed.

People don't think about what they do every day, because it has become a routine for them, I like to use performance art to interact with people and spaces. It is a way to connect with people, or to interject [something into] their routines so that people can be critical about established norms and contemplate the way they act in certain spaces.

Performance art has undergone a lot of censorship due to its public nature and its potential to engage with wider audiences. What are your views on the censorship or regulation of performance art?

I don't think there is a need to specifically set a standard for reviewing performance art. The artist should measure the limits of her own behaviour and what boundaries she wants to challenge. She also needs to bear the consequences of her own actions. There's no need for double standards [for artists] because we already have laws on how to live in a society. But there are grey areas. This is the space where performance art comes in.

Jennifer's workspace in the living room. The shelves are lined with her books, art materials and her husband, Gan's paintings.

WORKING PROCESS

Can you talk about your working process? How do you start?

As mentioned, usually I start with some questions that I want to answer. And I use my art to find the answers. I like to explore various issues on human desire and human nature. My art is a journey that tries to answer my own questions about these subjects.

I am a multimedia artist, so it depends on my mood. Sometimes, I like to walk around the neighbourhood or cycle around. It depends. Other days I will plan my artworks and sketch them out first. Sometimes, I record the surroundings with a camera or video my own body. So, it's intuitive and experiential.

Do you consider your work very personal?

It's personal, but I approach painting and video very differently. With painting, I find it to be a very physical act so, often, I just paint without prior planning. With my video work, usually I have some ideas I like to explore. I am interested in subjects like sexuality, desire, and impulse…

Can you elaborate on this?

I may think about how the body affects the way people react to it. Each body has a different physical contour and this elicits different interpretations of the body and contrasting reactions or impulses towards the body.

Or I may think about how one might handle things differently being a woman… in terms of being in control of the body. Recently when I was pregnant, I experienced a distancing from the body. I realize the body is stronger than 'me'. The body reacts faster than the mind. I consider how the body adapts to the things surrounding it. When the pregnancy process was completed, so to speak, I needed to find 'me' again. When I found myself, I was a little different than before the pregnancy. It is very difficult to explain in words. But I use the video as a way to help navigate my journey as a woman.

What is the process like when you use video?

Sometimes I have a recurring image in my mind that I need to express in different ways. I like to use my body to deliver my message and to express myself. For example, I have a strong image of a body separated by a line that runs across in the middle [indicating a vertical line

from head to toe]. I have the urge to express this. I may use a lipstick to then replicate that on my own body and experiment with it and let that process lead me… see how that works.

Do you think of yourself as a woman artist?

I am first human. But I am aware that I am a woman within a social world and, therefore, having social functions as a woman. Life is more important than art, not the other way round. When you live your life well, your art will follow. I also use the video as a medium to think about the idea of being a woman and what that means in society.

You mentioned that you also write poems.

I find that I express myself better in poetic form. I find it difficult to write in sentences and to verbalise my thoughts, sometimes. But, somehow, I am able to write it down as a poem. Sometimes I just type it out on my phone.

Notes

1   國立臺灣師範大學附屬高級, 師大附中 - Shī Dà Fùzhōng (Affiliated Senior High School of National Taiwan Normal University)

2   國立臺北藝術大學

3   Xu Yi Ting, also known as Eating Xu.

'This used to be a large canvas but I found that it was too large for me, so I cut it up until it was a size that I was comfortable with.' Jennifer's abstract drawings and paintings often relies on spontaneous decisions and experimentation, in contrast to the detailed planning behind her performance or video work.

Turning the living room of her house into a studio space, Jennifer says she needs ample space because she likes to lay her works on the floor and work while moving around them, without an easel.

ISE a.k.a ROSLISHAM ISMAIL
THE INDEFINABLE ART OF BEING

Ise's art explores a diverse range of subject matter, such as travelling, meeting new people, making friends, as well as social customs, family histories, exchange of knowledge and cultural traditions. His art takes the form of drawings, paintings, collages, found objects, installations, and performances – as well as a combination of these forms – to create what may be called participatory art.[1] Ise himself does not describe his own work as participatory; however, he considers the processes of participatory art like dialogue, interaction and engagement with the audience, to be aspects that he personally values. His art process is characterised by a collaborative style of working, in which he employs a team of friends to produce various parts of the project, while he spearheads the artistic direction and vision.

Ise also enjoyed a stint as an art teacher in Institut Teknologi MARA (ITM) before launching into full-time art practice. When he first started out as an art student in Kota Bahru, he was interested in drawing and painting. However, he gradually felt that those modes of expression were not always the best ways to present his ideas, as they did not allow him to interact with the space and people in the way he believed necessary.

Soon, he began to realise that the artistic process itself is as relevant and meaningful to him as the art object or image produced. From then on, he began to acknowledge the significance of the art process by documenting

it and including it as part of his final work. Pursuing this direction, his work started to fully incorporate non-traditional media and the artistic process itself, resulting in unexpected collaborations and thought-provoking forms of art.

An excellent example of this approach is demonstrated by his 2010 work, a one-and-a-half year long project for the Singapore Biennale, which started out with questions about how people lived in Singapore. This project led Ise into people's houses, where he interviewed them and looked in their refrigerators to see what they bought and consumed as a family. The final artwork comprised a film documentation of the actual shopping for food, and the installation of six refrigerators with real food specifically bought and arranged by the respective families. In the exhibition entitled *Secret Affair*, Ise provided a glimpse into the lives of these Singaporean families through what he called the 'secret box' – their refrigerators. While the artwork allowed him to present aspects of a typical family's eating habits and norms, the act of getting to know these families at a personal level over time was an integral part of the process that informed his direction and final presentation of the work.

Such works, while not controversial in content, were often met with uneasiness in terms of their validity as a form of art. His works provoked the age-old question, 'Is it Art?' as well as considerations of where 'art'

In memoriam: ISE
(1972 – 23rd July 2019)

To Ise, who brought people together and inspired them to create original works of art together. He carved out his own path in a sometimes ungenerous art world, reminding us that while it is difficult to swim against the current, it is also necessary when it is the only honest way available.

Drawing continues to be a source of pleasure for Ise, who keeps journals of sketches throughout his research process. He says, it's the best way of recording and organising his thoughts.

Left: A sketch of the layout and design for *Operation Bangkok.*

Right: *Operation Bangkok* exhibition, Bangkok University Gallery, Thailand. 2014.

ISE

begins and ends. He jokes that sometimes people think he doesn't do anything, because he lets others produce different parts of the work for him. But his process requires a different kind of work: laborious negotiation and long hours of conversation with strangers and friends, which often entail much uncertainty. This requires a flexible approach towards work and a more elastic definition of art. Ise embraces this ambiguity as a natural part of his journey in art, and looks for partners who understand this process. Ise calls his collaborators 'Superfriends'. These are partners who want to share his art experience and vision with him.

While it is hard to argue for the aesthetic criteria of such collaborative art, Ise says, in the end, it is up to you, the audience, to decide whether or not something can be considered art. What is important for him, is to be himself and to do what he knows best. The synergy of working together is what he ultimately finds beautiful.

GROWING UP

What were your first exposures to art, growing up in Kota Bahru?

When I was a little boy, I really loved drawing. I loved art but the education system in Malaysia – the teaching of art in public schools – kills our love for art. So I didn't do any art when I was in school. Even during SPM,[2] I did not take art as a subject. My mother passed away when I was 17, when I was doing SPM. My father's sister, a good

friend of my mum, also passed away exactly one month after that. And then, my father got really sick, as he had kidney problems.

My life was really a mess at that time – I didn't care about anything, so my SPM was ruined. I wanted to go to ITM but it was not possible because firstly, I did not take art [as a subject in school] and secondly, my exam results were really bad. So, the only thing I could do was to take care of my father – but I'm proud of that, actually… I had to get a car license and take him to the hospital three times a week. So, that's what I was doing [after high school].

Did you finally obtain your SPM?

If I wanted to register and take the exam, I had to go to class. So I went to night classes. Because I was the youngest at that time (when I finished SPM)… I started to hang out with a different generation of people. That's when I was first exposed to people outside of my small circle.

There was one guy at night class who was really good at drawing. So, I asked him, 'Wow, where did you learn this?' and he said, 'I learned it from the Kelantan State Gallery. There's a class there.' Then he said, 'You just go, yeah? Every Thursday, there's a class.'

I remember I bought some five cents paper at the *kedai runcit* (grocery store). And some Guitar [brand] poster colour paints with a cheap Chinese brush. It surprised me, when I went there… everybody was doing the measuring thing [mimics the artists' 'sight' method of measuring proportion with the pencil and thumb and laughs]. They are crazy, professional.

I remember when I took my paper out, everybody in the class just stopped their drawing and laughed at me because of my five cents paper… you put water on it and it goes …*bzzkkk!*

But I stayed on until I finished. As I was walking home, it's like the devil and the angel were in my head. One said, 'It's enough *lah*. You cannot be humiliated by people like this.' And the other said, 'No, you should fight!' Then I stopped, and I went back to the class.

The teacher was really shocked that I came back, maybe he thought that I wanted to punch him. But I just asked him, 'What kind of paper does everybody use?' And he said, 'Basically, it's like Tulip [brand] drawing paper, you can buy it at a stationery shop over there.' Then I said, 'What about the brush?' and he said, 'I sell these brushes.' Because he's Thai, he had bought all the brushes from Thailand, so I just bought his brushes.

And then I asked him, 'What's the best way to learn?' I remember, him saying, 'Copy. You have to copy.' I said, 'Copy what?' And he said, 'The Malaysian Watercolour Society catalogue is there. Take it.'

So, I took that Watercolour Society catalogue, brought it back and stopped at the stationery shop to buy the Tulip paper. Then I copied for 2 weeks [everyday]. After 2 weeks I went back to the class with two rims of drawing, and it shocked everybody.

LEARNING PROCESS

You were teaching art for a while after you graduated from ITM. Why did you stop and how did that experience shape your own thinking about art today?

Okay, it's a long story. Even though my results were really bad when I graduated, suddenly I got a call from one of my teachers in the first year department, because he opened a branch in Kelantan. He asked, 'Ise, would you like to come?'

You were offered a position as a teacher in ITM, Kelantan?

Yeah… and for me, it was really like a dream actually. I never imagined that ITM would call me. So I started teaching part-time. I was teaching the first-year students. I had 120 students. I really enjoyed teaching and I think I am a good teacher – but people don't always understand what I'm trying to do with the students.

ITM had sent me a letter for an interview for a permanent position in Kelantan… it was a mystery to me why they had asked me. But I thought that I should go for the interview. They said, 'Okay Ise, you just say yes and we will sign this and you can go for the second interview tomorrow. Take your English exam and we will send you to U.K. for your Masters.' And then I said, 'No.' And so they were really pissed off. They asked me why. I said, 'I want to be an artist.' And they said, 'What kind of artist?' I said, 'I don't know.' It was 2001, I didn't know what kind of artist I wanted to be. …I just wanted to be an artist.

They said, 'We are all artists.' I said, 'I don't want to be like you.' They said, 'What do you mean?' I said – I don't know, it just came out – I said, 'I don't want to be a "by-request" artist.' 'What do you mean by-request?' I said, 'By-request means you have a good salary and you claim you are an artist, but you only work when you get a letter from the gallery. That means you have been requested on paper to make work. So, it's "by request" and I don't want to be like that.'

So, they kicked me out of the room…

Later, I got a letter from ITM that my part-time teaching was cancelled. So, I had to start my freelance again. Start from scratch again. It was quite miserable in 2001 and 2002. But then in 2003, I got my first invitation for a residency in India. That changed the whole direction of my life.

How did your residency in India change your artistic direction?

Although it was very studio-based, that experience made me realize how big the network of artists is around the world. I met a Kenyan artist, an Indian artist, a Pakistani artist, and that's when I had the idea for the *Parking Project*.

Then in 2004, when I was invited to Ruangrupa [an art residency in Jakarta]. That totally changed the way I work; even now when I talk to people, I say that my school of thought is 'Ruangrupa'.[3]

Ise performing with
Ruangrupa at the
7th Asia Pacific Triennale,
Australia 2012.

ISE

Can you explain Ruangrupa's school of thought?

When I arrived in *Ruangrupa* …there was nothing there [laughs]. There was just a computer for editing! Every day we just talked, wake up in the morning and… talk again. Then at night, go to parties, and come back very late. That's how it was for two months actually.

But, during the last part of the residency, Ade [Darmawan] – that's the director, and my good friend – he said 'Okay, tomorrow we have an open studio.' And that surprised me. Everybody can pick up anything as a piece of work and talk about it. So, the training in Ruangrupa emphasised the process, in contrast to the conventional approach that I learnt from ITM, which was about the final result. So, I learnt that you can actually pick up any object and talk about it, and that talking was part of the whole artistic process.

In 2006, when I got my residency in Sydney, I manipulated these two experiences in my artwork: the final work was inspired by the studio space in India; and then I made a book about my process which was inspired by my experience in Ruangrupa. [My book] is a diary, called *Keluar 90 Hari* (Go out for 90 Days)[4] I documented the process: who I met and what I've been through the whole three months [in Australia].

In a way, isn't your art as much about the experience of being an artist as it is about the process?

I don't know if it's a good thing or not, but that's a way [for me] to survive. Some people do not understand. They think that I'm from a rich family. No, my [parents] passed away a long time ago, but [being on] the streets really made me think about how to survive [as an artist].

I remembered that during my first trip [outside Malaysia], I backpacked. I didn't mind it, I just worked, and painted buildings and houses. When I got the money – 500 ringgit – I took a train to Chiang Mai to see an art exhibition. That's the effort that I take that people don't see. There are some lucky people in the world who get a solo exhibition right after they graduate, but not everyone is so lucky. I'm not one of the lucky ones in the way of the journey. I work hard and I face a lot of challenges. But I'm satisfied with what I'm doing.

SPACE AND PLACE

What made you move to this part of the city?

I stayed on the other side of Pandan Indah for 12 years. After graduating, I just stayed in Shah Alam with all my friends. … It can be very comfortable when we are in the zone with friends, but at the end of the day, I feel like I am actually not very productive.

Were you sharing a studio?

No, it's a house we were renting with four of my friends; two of them were teachers at that time in the university (UiTM). So our house was frequently full of guests. It's okay, it's good like that, but the problem started when too many guests kept coming.

I remembered we tried to enter the Philip Morris exhibition. We had to share the lorry to send the paintings to Balai [Seni Visual Negara].[5] So our house in Section 10 was the last stop. When the lorry came to our house, everybody had to rearrange the paintings in the lorry to fit our artworks. So, when we did that, it really shocked me: five or six paintings [in the lorry] looked pretty similar to what I was doing.

I'm very open, I'm not secretive, but things like [this] is too much now. So, I decided to move. Then, I had a fashion designer friend who had a studio in Pandan [Indah] and found me a small flat.

Ise in the living room of his studio/apartment as part of *Parking Project*, 2017, which was reinstalled in the Bangkok Art and Culture Center.

Parking Project has been conceptualized by the artist as a living space/installation that stimulates artistic discussion and collaboration.

The space is strewn with framed works from past and present, souvenirs from travel, knick-knacks, works in progress and a library of books and catalogues.

The door is covered with luggage tags from his travelling.

Ise's work station with his past drawings and collage work on the wall.

Framed works on display in his guestroom/gallery where artists, curators and friends have stayed overnight.

Langkasuka Cookbook Project, 2012, featuring recipes from his grandmother, her friends and neighbours. Ise remarked that the project is not just about food but about how we share these types of knowledge from one generation to the next.

the good scenery, but not for me. Better stay home in Malaysia. Because at the end of the day, I'm still in front of my computer, trying to arrange things.

Do you see residencies as an important part of the way you work?

Personally, yes. Because firstly, I don't have enough time and space to work. As a normal human being, you want to show your work, but in Malaysia, you don't really get the chance to do it. So I think it's very important for me to go out [of Malaysia] and run away from a system that will not accept what I do.

CURRENT PRACTICE

You've been producing an interesting body of work that has been difficult to categorise as 'art' in a conventional sense. For instance, you produced a cook book as part of your artwork when you were in Australia. Was that a challenge for you?

The APT (The Asia Pacific Triennial of Contemporary Art) commissioned me to do a work and I proposed the cookbook [*Langkasuka Cookbook Project*, 2012]. And because the museum had a department for publication, they sent it there for printing. When it came back to me, it was changed. They took out some drawings …they took out one page… we had a big fight. They didn't understand that, for me, the book was my artwork. I said that even if you changed 5% of my design, it's problematic. I said, 'You commissioned other artists to do their work?' They said, 'Yes.' 'My question is, do you touch up their painting when it has dried?' They said, 'No!' 'Same with my book… How dare you touch up my work?' In the end they printed 50 copies. They said that nobody will buy the book. I said, 'It's fine, but don't touch the design.'

We also had an artist talk with myself and the chef about cooking outside the museum, with the river as the background. It was very nice and we served the *sirap pisang*, the glazed banana, which became a dish in the museum for the whole biennale. One plate cost 22 dollars! I told my grandma and she said, 'You can buy a whole tonne of *pisang* (bananas) for that. Even more!'

So, during the talk, I [related what] I learned from my grandma, the 'old school'

When did you finally move to this current studio?

In 2015, suddenly the landlord said he wanted the flat back. I had so much stuff, I was panicking as I didn't have money. I thought, okay, I've got all my old drawings. So, I framed them up and made an open house. I just put them in a frame on the bookshelf. Then, we invited people to come. So, I earned a bit of money to move here.

Since networking is quite a big part of your job, do you need to stay close to the city so that you can stay in touch?

Yeah. Don't put me in the *kampung* (village), I will die [laughs]. No, actually, I'm from Kelantan.

Once I had a residency in Korea, they put me in the kampung. I couldn't do anything. Yeah, it's really hard. It's really hard. … because the way I work is different. There are artists who do painting, and they really enjoy

Secret Affair, 2011, Singapore Biennale. Right: One of the participants, an amateur photographer, stores his films in the refrigerator.

ISE

way. For example, she would say, 'You just cut the banana in the middle, with the skin on, and boil it to take out the bitterness,' or something like that. Then the chef who studied in a technical way would say, 'Oh, Ise is right. His grandma is right, because according to my study…' And the people were like, 'Wooo… wah!'

Then I just played around, I said to the restaurant head, 'We only serve 40 plates a day.' It's just a number, just for fun. And then, you know what happened? There was a queue! People had to book for days in advance.

Do you ask yourself, 'So how is what I'm doing art, and when is it not art?' And how do you come to terms with that?

A few days ago, a 'member' (friend) came for dinner. We threw a housewarming party, they think that's an artwork. No, I said this is just a housewarming! …or I put a photo on Facebook, and some people ask, 'Is this your new work?' No! It's just a photo! … So, in the end, I think I'm the artwork actually!

Do you find the whole set up of the gallery and the museum problematic? In a sense that it automatically sets up a divide between what is art and what is not?

When I go to Bangkok [for an art residency] I have to adapt, without thinking that it is a gallery or that it is the Bangkok Art [and Culture] Center. I have to do that. That's the place that I want to set up a house, my living room, so that's my way of breaking the stereotypical concept people have about how a gallery should look like.

Before I arrived, they got worried, they asked, 'When are you coming to Bangkok to set up the space?' I said, 'No worries,' because when I go there, when I'm shopping, that's me doing my thing. That's what you want, it's about how I'm setting up my own space… the project is about me [as an artist], my art process and my experience creating art.

So, sometimes it's funny, yeah. I have that kind of idea but at the end of the day, I just don't give a damn, actually. If you think this is an artwork, it's okay, it's up to you.

MATERIALS AND TOOLS

Would it be more accurate to say that you stay away from traditional materials, or that it doesn't matter to you what materials you use?

It doesn't matter for me. I'm not against painting. If the only way to express my idea is through a painting, then why not?

In my work in Singapore Biennale [*Secret Affair*, 2011], it's about finding different channels to do the same things. [In the old days] the artist goes to the market to buy the vegetables for still life and set it up to make a drawing. It's the same thing, I go to the market and buy these things, but where do I put it? I put it in the fridge as part of my work. So, in Singapore, families go shopping and they come home to put the things in the fridge.

Superfriends get together: Ise works with different teams of people who have flexible roles in different projects. Bob (Azami A. Rahman) (third from left) has been documenting Ise's work through photography, Zul (Zulkarnain Shaharudin) (second from left) has been involved in design, while Do Tuong Linh (right) is a visiting curator from Hanoi.

I ask my photographer to take the still life of the products. Or I can even do a painting or drawing of the still life… that would be nice too… But that's not the whole point, because the work is not all about the image. It's also about the process, the interaction, the connections with people.

Like for the cookbook [*Langkasuka*], I can hang the drawings of the cookbook anytime but it's meaningless in the space because it's not about the image. It's about the whole process. So, you have to have a book, you have to have a video…

But people here just want to see the image and they want to buy the image. So that's why I do sell a few of my drawings. But I only sell it to people who really understand what I'm doing. These friends are the ones who buy because they know the experience; they buy because they know the mark of my work and not because of the images themselves – not because the images are good.

WORKING PROCESS

Can you describe your typical day?

It depends, yeah… on a routine day, morning is quite quiet because most of my friends are working. In the afternoon and evening, we will be busy. I'm a morning person, I wake up early to work on whatever I can on the computer and other things [because] people still don't disturb me at that time. And then after 12 p.m., I've already done my thing, I can start dealing with people. My day is full of meetings, five or six meetings, with different [people] but for the same project. And then, once a week, we go out for dinner, my team, to recap what's happening.

Tell me about your work process. When you are brainstorming or conceptualizing your project, who's with you?

My favourite guy, the one I usually talk to, is Syed – Hanim's husband.[6] He's super genius! He's an engineer but I like him because he's a good writer. So, sometimes I just go to Ipoh, sit down with him and explain my ideas to him. He compiles what I say and then I can get what's inside my mind in writing, because I'm not really good at writing.

I also have an overseas team… I've been hanging out with this Indonesian gang. I have a good friend [studying] cultural studies in Jogjakarta. So, when I go online, I just chat with them.

What does your team look like now?

It's very flexible. For the Mori Art Museum project, we have the department of design, department of silk screen, department of purchasing, department of information. I just tell them what I want and they will provide me with it.

I have to be fluid with how I'm working because, if not, it would be impossible to work. So, for example, one of my friends works for the government and he works for the intellectual property department. I just email him or call him saying, 'I think I need that kind of information', and because he knows about the project, he is willing to help.

Ise holds an Open Studio to invite friends who are interested to buy his work, or just to come eat and hang out.

Then, there is one guy who will work on the fabrication so I have to follow him and instruct him about the kinds of things we need. Yeah, actually it's a tough job. But people always think I do nothing [laughs]. That's the problem. But I'm the one who has to...

You have to manage all the different teams!

I have to put it together. And so, the difficult part, the crucial part for each of my projects is to make sure each of them is on the same page, and that they are passionate about it. I have to explain to this guy, and this guy, and this other guy, the same way I explain to the curator. So, everybody starts to become excited and they feel like they belong to the project, not that they are being asked to do a job.

How important are the participatory aspects of your work? Do you think about how you can get your audience to interact with your work when you are conceptualizing?

I don't think about that when I'm doing the work. I just love hanging out with people. It's not about trends. It's about being with people.

For every work that I produce, it's like a blank slate. I need to go to the place to see it, smell it, get a sense of the place before I know what I want to do. It's a scary process because I don't know what I am going to do until I get there. So I don't see the point of producing something in KL for the residency. Because I might as well just stay in KL then. Instead I try to adapt to my new situation overseas and produce something out of that experience.

Do you have any kind of routine or process that helps you to stay motivated when you're working?

Yes! Superfriends! The only thing I like about KL are my friends. It's because of my friends that I'm still based in KL. I have a group of friends, not many, but they are the ones who enjoy these experiences with me.

But they have other jobs too. I told them, I can pay them... but don't let this be the main job....you can do whatever you want, but I just need a little bit of your time.

Notes

1   Participatory art emerged within the artistic mainstream during the 1990s, and is now recognised as a form of art where the audience is actively engaged in the artistic process.

2   The *Sijil Pelajaran Malaysia* (Malaysian Certificate of Education), equivalent to GCE O-Levels, certifies the successful completion of higher secondary education in Malaysian schools.

3   Ruangrupa (2008) is an Indonesian art collective based in Jakarta.

4   *Go out for 90 days (Keluar 90 Hari)* was republished as a visual essay in *Inter-Asia Cultural Studies*, Volume 9, Issue 3 (2008), Taylor and Francis.

5   Balai Seni Lukis Negara (National Visual Arts Gallery).

6   Syed Omar Husain, husband of Malaysian artist and writer Nur Hanim Khairuddin.

ELIAS YAMANI
EVERYDAY OBJECTS, ALTERNATE WORLDS

Elias is an artist who works with found objects. As a sculptor, he is trained to work with traditional materials such as wood and metal, however, he chooses to work with reusable, discarded or bought materials. He says that while many are puzzled by his choice of what may be viewed as waste material or commonplace objects, his attraction to them stems precisely from their quotidian qualities and relatability.

Since the early 20th century, artists have consistently turned to such commonplace materials as a resource for diverse reasons. For some, this turn is a protest against elitist categorizations of high and low art; for others, it was borne out of necessity due to the unavailability of art materials, while there are also those who view it as a necessary detour to invigorate prevailing mainstream art practices. Elias says that in his art practice, all of these reasons partly applies to him.

While many art terms such as assemblage, found object, readymade or bricolage may be used to describe his work, he is especially fascinated with the notion of bricolage and its improvisational aspects. He identifies himself as a *bricoleur* – having the ability to utilise whatever resources that may be at hand to produce art.

Elias is quick to point out that he does not strive for illusionistic artworks – such as portraits or landscapes produced by conventional media. He has felt increasingly distanced from conventional art materials like paint, canvas, metal, wood or clay, as they have no relevance in his life in the city.

In contrast, he is naturally drawn to the materials which he comes into contact with every day, such as stationery, machinery or usable leftover parts of such objects.[1] So instead of asking *why* such found objects are privileged in his art-making. He asks, 'Why not?' He explains that these materials usually have intrinsic tactile qualities that make them highly appealing. What interests him is the substance itself – its malleability, physical qualities and the meanings that may be attached to it. Thus, his selection of materials is often based on intuition or a reaction to its physical characteristics rather than being about how the material can express a preconceived idea for an artwork.

One of his artistic stimuli comes from the idea of world-building – the process of creating alternate universes or fictional worlds that consist of imaginary peoples, cultures and geographies, as well as working within hypothetical sets of physical or metaphysical laws. World-building in literature and film, is something that continues to inspire many of his works. He uses world-building as a method of inquiry about the world we inhabit, to make explicit the assumptions we hold about nature, culture and society. He notes that only when we start from a premise of the question 'What if…?', can we resist the idea of pre-determined destinies, thereby opening our minds to more possibilities

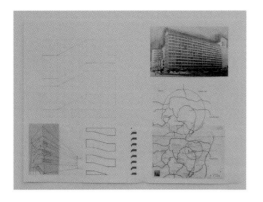

Exploratory studies: designs are drafted out on paper and materials tested using small scale models.

ELIAS YAMANI

and alternative ways of functioning in the present world.

It is not surprising that his artwork resembles semi-identifiable objects fallen out of an alternate universe – partly-recognizable, but combined in peculiar configurations. There is no identifiable narrative. Rather, objects are presented as they are. They are not symbolic and they do not refer to something else. They seem to assume new roles or purposes, and the audience is persuaded to offer various possibilities for these *new* objects.

As the founder of *Satu: Creative Collective* (2008), he has curated exhibitions with like-minded artists who look for different ways to reach audiences and to connect with those interested in their art.

Finding institutional spaces sometimes too restrictive, his role as a curator is partial especially to artists whose works may not be readily accepted in such establishments, and to those who need an alternative space to create experimental works. He emphasises that established galleries expect works that are 'finished' or conceptually complete and accompanied by well-defined rationales. Occasionally, an artist may produce a rationale merely to satisfy the needs and demands of the curator or the collector.

In reality, artists are often unsure of where they're going with a work. They may be in the midst of exploring a new path or theme and they might not always have neat explanations for these decisions. Even then, Elias feels that such works are still worth showing to the public, because this gives them a platform for honest feedback and dialogue. His work as a curator thus represents a current breed of artists who are stepping outside the conventional boundaries of art-making, to create non-elitist and non-exclusive spaces for art.

GROWING UP

When were your earliest exposures to art?

It was during primary school that I remembered being exposed to art. I went to a missionary school, St. John's [Institution] in Kuala Lumpur and I remember the many relief sculptures around the school. It was an old building and so we were surrounded by art. The floors had mosaics that featured our school houses. The teachers, too, were trained in art – they came from universities or the teacher's training college. So, they were very much interested in the arts. I still remember going for field trips to the National Art Gallery and attending film screenings in that primary school.

What kind of movies did you watch during those film screenings?

Popular movies like 'Smokey and the Bandit', Bruce Lee films, and even 'Jaws'! They used the old projectors to screen the shows at that time. I recall having very good exposure to the arts in general, not only in fine art but also in music. A lot of my friends were in the school brass band and it was a good experience.

How did your experience growing up shape your artistic choices today?

I grew up in KL – in the city, so my memories are of the sights and sounds of the city. So, for example, I don't go to fishing villages or rubber plantations or the beach, I don't go around picking seashells, or go to nature for inspiration [laughs].

But what I can remember is the construction of the city – the pounding of the metal and the lorries bringing all this stuff... so these are my memories, and because of that I relate better to man-made or industrial objects.

Elias remarked: 'Sometimes I'm lucky enough to find shop owners or carpenters like Lau here, who won't mind me using the space and looking through their leftover wood stock.' He was referring to his friend C.K. Lau, owner of J.K. Interior and Renovation, who allows him to use the space and leftover materials.

LEARNING PROCESS

Can you recall some of the milestones in your learning process?

Around 2003, I was pursuing my masters degree with [the late] Redza Piyadasa.[1] That programme was an eye-opener for me. Before I enrolled [for the course], I was already working for him as an assistant [in] a government-funded project – that was how I made a living while preparing for my solo. I found that what I lacked was knowledge and I needed access to books. It occurred to me that University Malaya would be a good place to gain that knowledge. I was talking to him casually when he asked me, 'Why don't you join the Masters programme in Visual Art?' So that's what I did.

Through the programme, I was exposed to the richness of Southeast Asia and the regional commonalities. I realised that many artists in the region were doing art that pushed the boundaries. It was inspiring in that sense, and I wanted to do something new as well.

Did your artworks change in any way as a result of that?

Perhaps my art-making process did not change, but I think my ways of seeing changed. Through the course I was exposed to postmodern theories, gender theories, *et cetera*.

I did not necessarily apply them directly in my artworks but, in general, it changed the way I viewed things. I also started an art collective called *Satu: Creative Collective*.

What were your objectives for starting this collective and what did you learn in the process?

I felt that, as an artist, it was difficult for me to get an audience. Perhaps it's because I was not doing paintings that were readily acceptable to the public. I realised I had to do it myself – if I wanted a show, I shouldn't be sitting around, waiting for someone to invite me to join them. I should just organise my own shows. So, I looked around for spaces that were open to having art exhibitions and gathered together artists who were interested to have group shows. Places like Alliance Française, Soka Gakkai and the Shah Alam Gallery were all very open to the idea. They also generate a different type of audience, which I like, such as expatriates or students, *et cetera*. And if they purchase the artwork, the owners of the space don't take a cut as 100% goes to the artist. We also publish our own catalogues.

Looking back, how has your art practice developed?

I try to be less superficial. I ask myself, 'What is my reality?', 'What materials carry

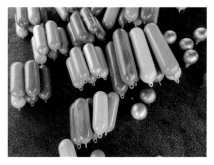

Teratai during the low-tide (Pulau Ketam, 2017). Elias explained, 'We decided to use floats as our material because we could find them in volume at Pulau Ketam and it was cheap. When we put them together, they look like teratai (water-lilies).'

ELIAS YAMANI

meaning for me?' And then, I go on from there. Previously, I was also less confident about my practice, but now I realise that I cannot do something just to be accepted. I can only do something because it is relevant to me.

SPACE AND PLACE

Where is your current working space?

I don't really have a proper studio. My studio is really a porch [*laughs*] and my room. I currently don't have the luxury of having a separate space, so I make use of what I have. I treat my studio like a lab where I have this trial and error process going on, so it's an important space. But when your studio is also your home, you get distracted with running errands and other things. But if you go to a proper office, people know you're in your office and they cannot disturb you. Something as simple as that, but it makes a big difference. So, I'm working towards separating my work space and personal space. In this area, residencies are helpful for artists like me.

You previously shared a studio and now you work alone, so what are the differences and which do you prefer?

I don't think I like having company in my studio. At a certain point in my work process, I need to be alone so that I can focus. If people visit for a short period of time, it's okay. But living and working together, for me personally, it's a distraction.

So how do you like working in a residency where you have to interact with others?

I had this experience when I did a project under the Sasaran Association[2] and also their splinter group, the Pulau Ketam Art Association.[3] They give you a studio but the studio is totally out of your comfort zone. I have no choice but to really adapt to the space and environment as soon as possible, because I have to work within a time frame of between three weeks to one month.

There are living quarters and also an area where you can produce work. You have to make use of what they have there. The format is like a residency or a workshop. The intention is to produce works on site, and to make the process open to the community so that they can see how the works are made. This opportunity broadened my views about the relationship between art and the community.

How did the environment affect your work?

I was challenged to see what materials I can use on site. I tried to take advantage of the space. I felt like I had the opportunity to expand my work in terms of skill and scale.

Because it was community-based, the studio could be in a different location every time. I love that concept of the studio being transported everywhere. Whereas in the conventional studio, the artists work mostly in isolation. It is held during the school breaks so that students can join in the project. The volunteers are also from the local schools around the area. Many artists live with the families of the communities, who open their houses to visitors during the art festival.

What are the advantages of having this type of mobile studio?

This approach encourages more cooperation between the artists and various parties, who are not working within the field of art. Like, for example, the volunteers are not from art schools and the administrative committee are not artists either.

Who is the community?

Well, in this case, they are mostly fishermen, of course!

How do they respond to your work?

They love it! They ask me, 'What are you doing?' Their response to my work, I have to say, is fresh, and I appreciate that because they don't have any preconceived ideas about art. It's good. You know, if you go to Sasaran, it's very interesting... You can go and see the *makcik jual nasi lemak* (the ladies selling coconut rice), they can talk about art too, 'Oh, this is installation... oh, this is sculpture.' As an artist, I appreciate that. The fact that my work is being seen by other people outside of the usual art circle, especially the younger generation of school kids. We bring the 'gallery' to them, rather than getting them to come to the gallery.

CURRENT PRACTICE

Tell me about your current work

I recently took the opportunity to visit Hong Kong to get inspiration and expand my horizons for research. There were two expos at that time, *Art Basel* and another local exhibition. It was fascinating and I made it a point to walk around the city by purposely staying in the outskirts of the city centre. It was good to gain a first-hand visual experience of how they live. The city is extremely congested

and people there have to live in very tight spaces. This work was produced immediately after I came back. I was walking in the back lanes and saw all the aircon compressors lined up at the back of the buildings. It reflected the congestion and the way of life in the city. So, in the work, I tried to capture the sensations of confinement, pollution and control by using real parts from actual air conditioners.

How do you select your subject matter?

I don't have a specific subject matter, but right now I'm interested in the concept of urbanisation. My work does not have a narrative, but in my current work I ask questions like, 'What are the effects of living in a modern city?' or 'Why is it that some still hold on to traditional attitudes while living in an urban, modern environment?'

I am also intrigued by the concept of world-building. I am influenced by films like 'Alien' (1979) and 'Blade Runner' (1982), both directed by Ridley Scott which are very futuristic. Or films like 'Space Odyssey' (1968) and 'Mad Max' (1979). In all these films, I am interested in how the director proposes alternate universes, and how he visualises these worlds and make them 'real' to us, to such an extent that it makes us rethink our current interpretations of things.

Can you give us an example?

Like in 'Alien', the film is not just about a different life-form, but rather, it's the representation of this form which twists our understanding of gender. The idea of a man struggling to give birth to another, makes me think about what happens if a man changes his sexuality in this way – having the ability to give birth [laughs]! It changes our traditional understanding of gender. There are many TV series now which

Projek 2 (AirCond), 2016, mixed media, 90 x 14 x 92 cm.

Lanjutan, 2011, found objects: fluorescent light on car hood, 6 x 4 ft.

ELIAS YAMANI

Left: The basic drill, grinder, circular saw (above) and jigsaw (below) are the only expensive electrical tools Elias invested in.

Middle and right: Part of the process Elias appreciates is scouting the back lanes of the city in search of new materials.

propose make-believe societies that expose or magnify fundamental aspects of our actual societies. Like 'Black Mirror' (2011) which talks about the dependence on technology and the hypothetical scenario if we were to push this idea to the extreme.

I am also interested in the idea of the bricolage and how as a *bricoleur* I can connect materials and ideas which do not normally exist side by side. As a process, it shares some aspects of retrofitting which is what I like to do in my work. In the futuristic worlds of Ridley Scott, you won't see new buildings, but rather old buildings that are retrofitted with new components. That is very interesting to me. So, in my work I love using old materials which are combined with bought material to create 'new' objects.

Are your artworks social commentary?

No, I wouldn't say that. When I first started practicing art, most people were painting and producing traditional sculpture, apart from a few artists. But I just had a natural love for working with different objects – how to shape them, refine them, juxtapose them.

But later on, I realised that perhaps I preferred found objects to the so-called conventional materials, because traditional painting is illusionistic. And I wasn't interested in creating illusions. For me, the material itself carries a meaning. So why shouldn't we just use the actual materials or objects instead of painting or sculpting an illusion of the object?

So, I started to explore how we respond sensually to materials. I remember thinking in high school that people are making extraordinary things. I was a fan of art from the beginning, intrigued by the world of creativity, whether they were writers, artists,

filmmakers or designers, I was inspired by this group of people. And I wanted to make objects of art.

MATERIALS AND TOOLS

Where do you source for materials?

Conventional shops, hardware shops as well as stationery stores. For example, in Penang I go to Lorong Kulit to get all this junk material. There is a lot of variety and it's cheap. Other than that, I can just get some from the art schools. Sometimes students have leftovers from their projects. People also leave discarded material by the roadside.

In KL, there is an abundance of material. Sometimes you go to Ikea, there are display boxes like containers for glass or mugs that have been thrown away.

As a student of sculpture, you were familiar with traditional materials and you used them during your school days. When did you stop using conventional materials and why?

Yes, as a student I did use 'normal' materials like metal, Plaster of Paris, clay, wires, maybe parts of wood for carving. I learned basic techniques for carving, welding, casting, *et cetera*. But somehow, I gradually lost interest in all those materials and traditional methods. I feel that they are no longer adventurous.

At what point did you feel this way?

After I graduated and came back, I really did not have the proper facility to practice as a sculptor, as I previously had while I was in school. But I had the desire to make works, and knew I had to find other alternatives. This meant that I had to make use of what I had. At that time, I did have some basic materials that I bought along the way. Like the drill, grinder and the jigsaw. The very minimum.

I also considered the fact that I chose to live in a residential area – I have neighbours. Techniques like metal welding is out of the question. So, I think this process developed because I was trying to work within my limits and my means. But now I also find that this process is more exciting than traditional sculpture because the possibilities are endless.

Do you have a particular process for selecting material?

Not an actual process, but I do need to have some attraction to the material. That is the first thing that makes me pick it up. However, I also sometimes use another approach, which is in reverse, maybe it doesn't have any immediate attraction, but I just pick it up anyway so that it may become useful later on.

But with found objects, you do need to plan in advance, technically speaking. The major issue with such objects is the sustainability – whether or not it is going to last, because you don't know how old these objects are. Some have been left out in the open for a long time, especially things you pick up from the streets which have been exposed to the elements. So how do you sustain it? If you don't do it, it will be a waste of your time.

WORKING PROCESS

Describe your work process.

I jot down my initial ideas on paper. I do some drawings and write notes about the types of material I'm thinking of using. Then I look for the actual material to make a model of the actual work.

Let's say I want to do an assemblage, I do a miniature assemblage so that I can identify how to solve problems. That way I can imagine solving it first on a small scale before I do it in actual size.

Then I do secondary sketches, where I consider various materials that I can use… maybe fabrics, sponges, scrubs. I test it out first. Like with acrylic sheets, I may spray it first and see how the effect turns out.

What are some considerations on how and where the work will be exhibited?

The work and the space need to complement each other. Also, if I organise a group show, then there needs to be a binding element that can hold the works together in one space. They could work with very contrasting materials but they still need a point of reference.

Do you also consider the people who may buy your work?

Not necessarily, but if I'm working on a special commissioned work, the person who commissioned the work would have to come and visit to take a look at the work midway, because they need to see the progress.

This happens also with exhibition projects where we need to have discussions on the direction of the exhibition. That is also something I love about the process. I appreciate the exchange of knowledge and their company and conversation. As an artist, I cannot be isolated so much, and when I have some ideas, I need to talk to people and get their opinions.

Elias was happy to discover reusable laminated plywood in abundance, 'These are half-inch thick, good quality and lasting. You can make all kinds of structures with it.'

Notes

1   Redza Piyadasa (1939–2007), was an artist, art historian, art educator and curator, and a pioneer in the field of Malaysian art in more ways than one. In 1974, he held a seminal art exhibition called 'Towards A Mystical Reality' with fellow artist, Sulaiman Esa. He co-authored one first academic introductions to the practice of modern art in Malaysia, 'Modern Artists of Malaysia' (1983) with T. K. Sabapathy. He was also an art columnist in the 'Business Times' between 1992–96, covering topics on art history, art practice, art patronage and other related subjects.

2   Sasaran Art Association (Persatuan Kesenian Sasaran) is a non-profit organization located in Kuala Selangor, a district north of Selangor state, Malaysia. Spearheaded by artist Ng Bee, Sasaran held its inaugural International Arts Workshop in 2008, and has since attracted artists and visitors from all over the world via art festivals that foster community engagement with art.

3   The Pulau Ketam Art Association (2014) is a non-profit organization located off the coast of Port Klang, Selangor, Malaysia. It replicates the success of the Sasaran art festival with an added focus on cultural tourism.

EIFFEL CHONG
UNCOVERING LIFE'S DISGUISES

As an artist who works with the medium of photography, Eiffel remarks that the camera has helped him gain new lines of sight. Entranced by the chemical processes of developing prints in a darkroom, he fell in love with photography as a student and thus began his journey to rediscover the world through the lens of his camera. Since then, photography has transformed his views on life and enabled him to see through its many disguises. His work articulates unique unique viewpoints and diverse subjects such as the the development of urban spaces, the treatment of wildlife, the nature of man and the impermanence of life.

Unlike the drawn or painted image, photography is often charged with the added complexity of being regarded as a reliable record of objects, personalities, places or events. It seems to be inherently authentic due to its historical use as a medium of documentation. However, today, this is no longer the case. Photography captures life simultaneously as 'real' and 'made up'. This paradox is artfully expressed in Eiffel's work.

His approach towards photography is tempered by his experience of living in urban Malaysia. With Eiffel's restrained approach, less is always more. In contrast with photographers who employ extensive staging or heavy digital manipulation, Eiffel keeps his photographs straightforward and uses natural lighting. This technique is reflective of his view that life itself provides situations and environments that are often 'unreal' and fabricated. The absurdities and deceptions of real life prove to be intriguing subjects in Eiffel's work.

In the series entitled *Institutionalised Care*, he captures various spaces in a hospital featuring such paraphernalia as beds, chairs, clocks and medical apparatus. There is a stark absence of activity. These are familiar spaces, and they relate to discomfort and disease. Yet without human presence, they seem to say so much more than just pain and suffering. His title leads us to ask the question of what happens when the act of caring becomes institutionalised. In his images, we begin to discover a nuanced answer to the question. These images visually describe detachment, loneliness and artificiality – characteristics in conflict with the notion of care. This tension is heightened by his strategic use of colours and clinical composition.

Eiffel also acknowledges that the practice of photography is marked by rapid change in technologies and materials. Finding good printers to work with is thus crucial to his practice. He is grateful to be working with a company[1] that houses one of the largest digital printers in Southeast Asia. What helps him most is the technical support he gets from his printer, who is himself a passionate photographer. Together, they solve printing challenges and enjoy the process of producing technically perfected photographs.

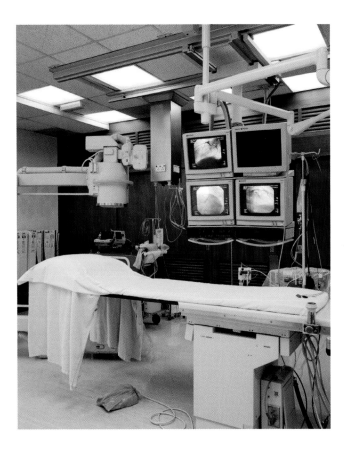

Left: '18', from
'Institutionalised Care' series,
2007.
EIFFEL CHONG

Right: 'Pulau Bintan', from
the 'Seascape' series, 2012.
EIFFEL CHONG

Stylistically, Eiffel says that he was inspired by the Düsseldorf School of Photography, birthed by influential photographer couple Bernd and Hilla Becher, who photographed thousands of industrial structures in Europe. Eiffel appreciates their ability to say something profound about society through simple subject matter and meticulous techniques. He notes their documentary approach that is both impersonal yet engaging; emphasising the formal qualities of purely functional buildings. By doing so, they changed the way people looked at such mundane edifices.

Like the Bechers, Eiffel proposes a new way of looking at the familiar, through the subtle interplay of the aesthetic and the documentary approaches in photography. He fuses these two approaches to reframe ordinary interiors, ever present objects around us and everyday landscapes. His pictures of the horizons in the series called *Seascapes* captures clear skies and the expanse of the sea. These images are familiar to most of us. Yet, his understated aesthetic heightens our senses. The sensitive rendering of light, colour, texture and austere compositions defamiliarise these scenes, so that we can begin to appreciate them differently as abstract images and distant borders.

In photography, our natural lines of sight are interrupted by the camera momentarily, to cause a break in the habitual ways by which we view the world. This momentary disjuncture is what gives photography its power to decode what's happening around us. For Eiffel, it has helped him uncover life's many disguises, and laid bare the ironies, contradictions and ambiguities within it.

GROWING UP

Can you remember your first exposure to art?

I wouldn't say that there was anything major during my childhood, but perhaps it was just some little things coming together. Like during my schooldays, everyone liked to draw and doodle. I was that kid who loved to draw superheroes – for example, Ultraman etc. – and that went on until secondary school.

Most of my family members did not get involved in the arts. I remember that my dad had multiple jobs, one of which was being a part of a team which required him to create small models of houses. I do remember seeing all these small architectural models when I was young. My mom worked for a travel agency and later became a remisier and now she's a corporate coach.

After completing my SPM, I totally did not know what I wanted to do. 1 finally decided to enrol in a Graphic Design programme as I was interested in drawing, art and design, *et cetera*. Photography just happened to be a subject offered in that programme – that was when I fell in love with photography.

I feel very fortunate that my mom supported my decision to pursue photography and I don't take that for granted because the exchange rate between the Malaysian Ringgit to the British Pound back in 1998 was RM6.30 to £1, so that made it very expensive to study overseas [at the London College of Printing in 2002]. Also in 2001, the Sept 11 attack made it risky to travel overseas. When I look back on those days, I am really thankful that my mom had the faith to let me continue. I wouldn't be doing what I am doing today, if it were not for that.

LEARNING PROCESS

Can you recall some of the milestones that shaped how you work today?

When I was in college,[2] we were still using film and I was working with black-and-white film. I remember the feeling of anticipation in processing a roll of film and getting the results after spending so long taking the shots, then preparing the chemicals and processing it.

The dark room is a good analogy for our lives – in life, in order to get a good outcome, you need preparation and patience, and there is a lot of waiting involved. But when the image appears before your eyes, that moment is worth the wait. It was very satisfactory and that's when I thought to myself that I really wanted to do photography. So I left for the London College of Printing in the UK.

In the UK, there was a different school of thought. I was forced to change the way I work because they didn't recognise the artistry in my work. My tutors said that there was 'nothing to see' in my photos.

What kind of work were you doing then?

Back then, I guess I adopted a 'typical' style of photography as a student – my subject matter was rather straightforward, for example, Orang Asli,[3] waterfalls, beautiful flowers. So my first year there was a bit of a torture. I thought that what I did was good. I was proud of my work. I already had five years of experience. I was young. My tutors said, 'You should look at photos like these.' However, I thought nothing much of the photos that they referred to as 'good'. I began to think, 'What is happening here? Am I wasting my time?' I also thought, 'Maybe I shouldn't continue.'

What made you change your mind?

A friend sat me down and said, 'The reason you are there is to learn. If you insist on holding on to your beliefs and not on opening up, you will not learn anything new. There must be something they know that you don't.'

Well, that made a lot of sense [laughs]! So, I went back as a 'fresh' person. I started to get serious about knowing the environment better, for example, I listed down different lighting conditions: when it got dark, when it rained, when it was cloudy. I was forced to use the tripod there because it was cloudy most of the time, and I got used to doing that as a routine till today.

Who was your tutor?

Anna Fox.[4] Her work is very different from mine. She spent a lot of time 'changing me', expanding my mindset as a photographer. She was really patient. She did not try to change the way I take my pictures, but the discussions were always about the concept and how to match the style of shooting with those ideas.

The school focused on how to conceptualise rather than how to use the (photographic) equipment – that was something you were expected to pick up on your own. I realised then that I did not understand the different vocabularies of photography... If you are self-taught, you may tend to dismiss photographers who do not appeal to you without first trying to understand why they do what they do in a certain way. I might not like a photographer's work but now I understand the merits in the photograph.

Sign Board, Alam Suria. 2016.
EIFFEL CHONG

Road Sign, Georgetown.
2014.
EIFFEL CHONG

It was a light bulb moment for me – that is what photography schools can give you.

Can you describe the school of photography that influenced your direction or style?

London was very influenced back then by photographers who were well-known for snapshot diary-ish scenes, whereas the Germans tend to be more structured [in composition and approach]. Most of my classmates took more spontaneous 'snapshots' but I was more interested in the German School known as the Düsseldorf School.[5]

Düsseldorf photographers and visual artists Bernd and Hilla Becher, together with painter Gerhard Richter, started a school which introduced the idea of topology or topography. For example, they photographed industrial structures like water tanks or warehouses. Their compositions were arranged in a grid format, and displayed the obvious similarities in what were actually different buildings (in different locations). Stylistically, I preferred this approach, and was influenced by the way they used subject matter which are generally overlooked, to say something poignant about the societies that built them.

SPACE AND PLACE

Do you think growing up in the city impacts what you do today?

I've never actually stayed for long periods of time in the outskirts. Even when I was studying in London, I was constantly in the city, so I've never felt what it was like to 'miss' it. I realised I needed the cinemas and the bookstores. Besides these two things, I don't really need much else, but still, because of this, I need to stay in the city [laughs].

Do you have a studio?

Well, my laptop is my studio. And this printing house is my studio in that sense. This is where I come to print all my photos.

When I first graduated, I worked for a print company and I used to print a lot of work for UiTM students. There were all these fine art photography students who used to come in with all this weird projects and sometimes we have to troubleshoot and see how we can get the prints to come out right for them.

So I learned a lot about printing from there and I got to know the manager of this current printing house from that place. He is very passionate about photography and takes the time to help freelance photographers solve their printing problems.

CURRENT PRACTICE

What are you currently working on?

My current works are about the failed institutions in society. The idea evolved about three to four years ago when I started to see photographers documenting their own city. These are location-based works but I do not want my works to be documentary. I am capturing Malaysia but on my own terms. I don't want to document Malaysia [in general], but only things that appeal to me. The work started organically, without any planning.

I have always been an optimistic person but what I have seen in my country was slowly turning me into a pessimistic person. The country was ugly, the economy wasn't in a good state, things were broken everywhere. What's happening to my country? I started to see it as a failed institution. What made this series 'worse' was the fact that I did not go looking for these scenes. They are practically everywhere.

What captured your interest?

I remember seeing something funny when I was in George Town, Penang for a photo festival. I parked near a one-way street and saw a street sign hung upside down, but it was pointing the right way. They probably ran out of signposts or something [laughs]. It was 'very Malaysian', I thought. It was creative but it's also sort of reflective of how things don't really work over here.

Do you go to specific places for this, or just drive around?

Sometimes I drive around and sometimes I get lost. Getting lost is a good way to see new things. Let's say I'm driving north to Penang, sometimes I just get off the highway at Taiping and use the old road instead of the highway, to see what is happening there. If I get lost, I'll just explore a bit. If I don't see anything, that's okay too.

Why do think you are more attracted to outdoor photography as opposed to indoor?

I wanted to be a journalist when I was growing up. There's still a part of me that wants to be a journalist. Going out there, documenting what is there. I prefer to look at the world outside and look at – well, it may sound a bit cliché – things that 'speak' to me, things that I can start to have some kind of relationship with.

Are you interested in local politics?

My work is not about that. I want to look at people in general, humanity as a whole and the institutions we build and how they fail us. For instance, my work on the Malaysian police is not exactly about Malaysia, but I think it coincided with what was happening here politically, so it was interpreted along political lines. But actually my friends in Thailand or Philippines are the ones who identified with it more than my local friends do.

I would like to go beyond the issues of gender, race or politics. I used to think, 'What if people don't understand [what I'm doing]?' Then I realised that it's impossible to come up with something that appeals to everyone. It is better to do something that appeals only to a certain group of people rather than change it to appeal to everyone.

Since 2015, Eiffel has been working with a Japanese-made Pentax 645Z which is a medium-format DSLR camera that comes with a 43.8mm x 32.8mm, 51.4 mega-pixel CMOS sensor. The larger size of the sensor allows more detail to be captured in an image. As Eiffel would explain to his students, 'It's like having a bigger piece of paper.'

Using a 'slow' camera makes it necessary to shoot with a tripod, in order to achieve more precise composition and lighting in natural settings, as opposed to controlled settings or spontaneous documentary-styled shots.

MATERIALS AND TOOLS

What was your first camera?

When I first started, I managed to borrow a Hasselblad which is a Swedish-made camera that has a 100-year old history. Back then, the technology was still new, so it was very expensive, it cost about RM90,000.

But I was fortunate enough to know Philip Ong the manager [of Shriro Malaysia] and dealer [of Hasselblad] in Malaysia. It was a fantastic camera. I asked him if I could loan it and, to my surprise, he allowed me to. In return, I put the logo of the camera on the catalogue of the exhibition. It was a demo camera, so priority was given to commercial photographers who would rent it for RM1,000 a day. There were low- and high-range ones, and I used one of the two units, the 50-megapixel ones.

When I could no longer use it (after Philip Ong left the company), my friend told me about an equivalent camera in terms of quality. He sold me his Pentax which is made in Japan. It cost me about RM30,000 for the camera, together with a few lenses.

What do you carry with you, when you go for your shoot?

When I was carrying around the Hasselblad, I was so aware that I could buy three cameras for the price of just this one. So, I either got my friend to accompany me or I packed along a pepper spray... So, if someone suspiciously comes a bit too near, I can protect myself, [with the] three-metre spray, grab my things and run like hell! But so far so good – never had to use it.

When I used a large format wooden camera, there never was a problem. I used to take photographs of abandoned places. There were drug addicts there, looking at me up and down, but when they saw the camera, they soon lost interest.

Do you digitally manipulate your images?

I often use only normal range lenses. This means that I don't really go for wide angle lenses. So what I capture on film is what the eye sees, there is very little distortion or manipulation. But sometimes I have to.

Like, if you look outside, the camera cannot capture everything you see – the details in the clouds and also the details on the road which is the darkest area. Your eyes can see that, but if I take a shot, I will either lose the details in the clouds or in the shadows. So you have to do some kind of manipulation.

Some people say, 'No, I don't do all these things, so I'm pure.' But do you know that using a different film will also give you a different result? So, when you make a choice to use certain types of films, your work is already a result of digital manipulation to begin with.

Nowadays anyone armed with a digicam or an iPhone can call themselves a photographer. What are your views on this?

Basically, photography is similar to other disciplines where, due to advancements in technology of equipment, there is easier access. But this doesn't mean that everyone is a professional. Everyone can cook but not everyone is a chef. Everyone has a word processor software in the computer, but not everyone is an author. Having said that, I think it's a great time for photography as there is more equipment for the professionals to explore. I have more choices of photo papers due to the booming market of photography.

What about paper selection?

For ink jet printing, you do get more paper choice because of newer technologies and a bigger market for a variety of paper surfaces. Different surfaces lend the photos a different feel. But I usually only work with C-type prints which are chemically developed.[6] For these, there are only two surfaces commonly available: gloss and matte. I don't use heavily textured paper because my work is not about the surface. I also want it to look like a photograph rather than, say, a painting.

WORKING PROCESS

What do you enjoy about your working process?

A lot of times people get upset with me for taking a photograph. They say, 'Oi! What are you taking?' But when I explain to them, 'Do you see this? I'm taking this,' then they are actually fine with it. It's scary at the time, because you don't know what to expect. But it all adds up to a spontaneous experience that you won't get from doing something else.

How many times do you usually print before you are satisfied with the results?

The print software that I work with on my computer is calibrated to the settings of the actual printer, so whatever appears on my screen is pretty much similar to what is displayed on the hardware on the printer's side. We do test strips and if I'm happy with them, we go ahead with the print. So usually one print is all it takes. The actual printing process only takes about 20 minutes.

What's a typical day like?

It really depends on the project. Previously, I was doing a series of seascapes so it's focused on the coastline of Malaysia. I travelled all the way to Melaka to catch the tide but when I arrived there, 'Where's the water?' [laughs]... So now I use this app that tells me when the tide changes every day. And because I need very bright sun and sunlight that is very calm, I use very slow exposure. So then, my 'ideal' shoot window would be from eleven-ish in the morning to about 4 p.m., depending on environmental conditions.

Sometimes people ask me, 'Do you get off-days during Chinese New Year?' But you can't look at it that way. For instance, the first day of Chinese New Year is the only time when there are no cars crowding the roads, so it was the best time for me to take the shots in the few places that I wanted.

So I guess there's no 'typical' day for me. Almost every day I have a different schedule. I work on a freelance basis on commissioned works, and I also teach part-time, so I have to plan my schedule around my classes. I have two to three days of teaching – it's quite balanced really.

Eiffel, using a colour corrected fluorescent light to check his test print. He says, 'What is important when I am checking the test prints is the consistency of the light. White should appear as white and that's sometimes hard to achieve without the right type of light.'

Checking the colour cast of the print from a series called 'False Face', which is based on the idea of man creating habitual masks. The test prints were printed on the same paper, on the same day, to ensure consistency.

Notes

1   J & A Imaging Station, Petaling Jaya, Selangor.

2   Limkokwing Institute of Technology, Kuala Lumpur.

3   Orang Asli is the Malay word for 'Original Peoples', a collective term referring to the diverse indigenous communities in Peninsula Malaysia.

4   Anna Fox is a British documentary photographer who focuses on the 'ordinary' as subject matter.

5   The Düsseldorf Academy of Art (Kunstakademie Düsseldorf) produced students whose collective work in photography since the 1970s became known as the Düsseldorf School or Becher School.

6. A C-Type (chromogenic) photographic paper is a light sensitive paper requiring the use of chemical processes. This technology combines the advantages of digital photography and editing, with high quality traditional photographic printing process.

AZZAHA IBRAHIM
BUILDING UPON OUR ARTISTIC PASTS

Azzaha is an architect, interior designer, researcher and artist. Growing up in Tumpat, Kelantan, Azzaha was surrounded by craftsmen and artisans, such as the *wayang kulit dalang* (shadow play master puppeteer*)*,[1] the *keris maker*,[2] the *wau maker*,[3] *and* the *batik* artist.[4] He grew to love the Kelantanese way of life as one where art is woven intrinsically into culture. Trained as an architect, he developed an appreciation for Malay architecture, especially the vernacular house on stilts, and works on the restoration and conservation of heritage buildings.

The architecture of the Malay vernacular house captures the familial cultural life of its inhabitants and also reveals their artistic sensibilities. Azzaha reckons that the natural harmony between culture and art, which was inherent in our traditional past, has been somewhat lost in contemporary times. Today, we often find ourselves living in built environments that are not only detached from our natural surroundings, but also disconnected from our cultural and aesthetic senses. In the past, the architecture of our houses encapsulated our artistic, social, cultural and religious thought. From the methods of construction to the selection of materials and the use of ornaments, each step of the process was emblematic of our relationship to the Divine and to each other.

Traditional building processes were not only symbolic but also upheld the archetypal principles of architecture – aesthetics and functionality. While these twin maxims are often celebrated today as legacies of the influential Bauhaus modernist movement, Azzaha reminds us that traditional architecture in the Malay Archipelago has always been an exemplary synthesis of beauty and purpose, art and craft.

To date, he has completed hundreds of architectural measured drawings of local traditional structures from the early 20th century, including the Malay house and *wakaf*,[5] as well as the Chinese shophouse and temples. As some of these structures are in a state of disrepair, such technical on-site drawings are essential documentation and references for future conservation.

His practice was what led him to appreciate the ubiquitous structure of the *wakaf*, which is an open pavilion made as rest stops for travellers, used since the pre-colonial era. The simplicity of its construction, according to Azzaha, gains little public interest. However, as an architect, he is enchanted by its graceful structure and stylised ornamentation. The *wakaf* is designed anthropomorphically – that is, the functional space is created with humanist proportions based on the height and movements of an average person, allowing the person or persons to sit and stand up comfortably. Its steep, double-tiered roof provides a comfortable ventilated roof space perfectly suited to humid tropical climates, and its large overhangs blocks off the glare from the sun. As Azzaha explains,

Two keris hilts with the Tajong (kingfisher bird) motif, believed to be from the early 19th century, *kemuning* (Merrillia) wood. A page from his sketchbook showing an illustration in pencil and watercolour tints.

Azzaha designed two traditional seals, one designating his full name and the other, an abbreviated symbol. Seals are often used in religious manuscripts to denote authorship of original and revised editions.

sometimes the *wakaf* is used for teaching, in which case, the split-level flooring allows the teacher to sit on the slightly raised level, facing the students on the main floor.

Azzaha also finds it exciting to work on the restoration of heritage buildings showcasing the creative use of timber in architecture. He believes that traditional knowledge in inventive and symbolic construction methods should inform the development of local contemporary architecture.

As part of the collective at Akademi Nik Rashiddin (Nik Rashiddin Academy), Azzaha teamed up with master woodcarver Norhaiza Noordin in conducting research work on Malay woodcarving, craft and architecture. It was at this academy that Azzaha became inspired to unearth the secrets of lost kingdoms such as Langkasuka.[6] Much time was spent gleaning through old manuscripts, examining traditional material culture and listening to oral narratives, as a way to piece together remnants of the past.

Art cannot be confined to disciplines like drawing, painting, craft or architecture, asserts Azzaha. These are merely categories within Western art historiography that have evolved as areas of study and specialization. He believes that we should continue to view art as a body of knowledge that inspires everything we do. It should inform the way we speak and our choice of words, or the way we serve our food or the way we write.

Azzaha is inspired to preserve traditional artistic knowledge by weaving it into contemporary forms in graphic design, interior design, architecture, drawings and paintings. He hopes that this will renew our interest to trace our own individual artistic lineages and make their presence felt in our contemporary practice.

GROWING UP

Can you remember your first exposures to art and how they have shaped your interests today?

My childhood environment in Tumpat, Kelantan, was filled with many people who practised traditional arts. Of course, I was influenced by them and was curious. I wanted to try everything. When I was in primary school, I was completely fascinated with the *wau* and I was making my own *wau* to the extent that my mother was worried about me [laughs]. I learnt from the master kitemaker, Awan Panjang, who was very skilful at making kites that not only looked beautiful but could also fly really well.

Then, when I was in secondary school, while waiting for my SPM results, I worked in a *batik* factory and became immersed in *batik* design. I told the boss of the factory that I would like to create my own designs and he said, 'If the designs don't sell, you will have to bear the cost!' I said, 'Okay.' At that time,

Azzaha making a sketch of a *keris* from memory at Pantai Sri Tujuh, Tumpat, Kelantan.

AZZAHA IBRAHIM

I did something crazy, I learnt how to skin and dry the *ular sawa* (python) and used the markings on its skin as a design pattern for the basis of my creations. In the end, they sold really well, and my boss said, 'Please create more!'

I also had neighbours who were *dalang* (master puppeteers) specialising in the art of *wayang kulit* (traditional Malay shadow puppetry), so I did pick up a thing or two about being a *dalang*. In order to be an excellent *dalang*, you need to be really well-versed in traditional idioms and *cakap-cakap orang Melayu lama* (archaic Malay sayings). A masterful *dalang* knows how to dramatise the dialogue and flesh out each character with historical and cultural anecdotes. Today, people don't understand this when they watch *wayang kulit* because they don't understand the sayings anymore.

It's the same, when you talk to someone about the *keris* (traditional Malay dagger), for instance. They will refer to it as *cakap kolot* (antiquated subject matter) and therefore unfashionable. Nobody is interested in the old stuff anymore. But if you present it via a contemporary medium like a painting, then perhaps people will take notice of it. That's part of what I'm trying to do – to revive an interest in cultures of the past by giving it a contemporary twist.

LEARNING PROCESS

After I graduated with a diploma in architecture, I did not feel like pursuing that discipline any further. I checked out the various courses in architecture and felt that I did not want to follow that 'template.'

Do you mean that the courses were too structured? What exactly were you looking for?

I was not sure. But I knew that I wanted to combine my love for art, culture and architecture. I believe that documentation is very important and I wanted to carry out my own in-depth research into areas that have meaning for me, not just produce something short-term, like a thesis that you submit just to get a grade or a certificate. So, I didn't want to take the 'usual' route pre-packaged for students. Instead, I wanted to determine my own direction and create my own path.

How did you start?

I remember that I spoke to Norhaiza, a protégé of Nik Rashiddin,[7] a master craftsperson in Malay weaponry. For about 10 years now, we've been conducting research together on architecture, woodcarvings and motifs that can be attributed to the ancient kingdom of Langkasuka.

I had three teachers, two of them have passed away, only one is left. Nik Rashiddin was one of my mentors and we were based at the Kandis Resource Centre, later known as Akademi Nik Rashiddin.[8] My experience there deeply influenced my continued interest in Langkasuka.

You have also started your own project on measured drawings. When and how did you start this endeavour?

I used to drive around and admire all these wooden traditional houses. I thought to myself that one day, all of these houses will be gone because they're constructed out of wood, so I should document them before they are destroyed. That is how I started this project with the traditional Malay house, sometime around 1998. My first drawing was of the *rumah tiang dua belas* (house of twelve posts), a very famous Kelantanese traditional house form, owned by Mohammad Dobah, also known as Tok Dobah.

The sunlit rear courtyard of the Chinese shophouse, in the process of being transformed into pantry/bar with a space allocated for a garden.

Right: Azzaha working on the first floor of a 1930s Chinese shophouse, now converted into his office, studio and gallery space.

What attracted you to that particular building?

It is like beautifully carved furniture. The walls, also known as *janda berhias*,[9] is unique to the traditional houses on the East Coast of Peninsular Malaysia. They reflect the social status of the inhabitants. If you look closely, the different parts of the building, the walls and the beams, are all decorated with intricate motifs. I am also interested in the symbolism of these motifs, such as the *daun bayam* (spinach leaves), *pucuk kacang* (bean shoots) – there are hundreds of them. Later I was inspired by this house to design an Anglo-Malay bungalow for one of my customers in Kelantan.

SPACE AND PLACE

Some people come here [to Kelantan] and think there is nothing much happening in this place, but there are so many places to explore. I can bring you on a *wakaf* tour and you will see such a rich heritage of traditional architecture.

In Kelantan, you can still see some people carrying the *keris* in a scabbard, [hanging out] at the coffeeshop. Where else in Malaysia would you see this? [laughs] It is becoming a rare sight.

What brought you to this current space?

I love the shophouse building and have always known that if I could find one, it would make an ideal space for me to work in. Why the shophouse? Well, I feel that since I'm working with traditional Malay architecture and artefacts, I wanted to juxtapose that with a contemporary space. So, I gave the interior a facelift to create that contrast between the modern and the traditional.

The top floor is the office space and the bottom is the gallery and future bar [laughs].

Are the works here for sale?

Not really. I'm not ready to sell my works at this moment, maybe one day. The other works are my friend's works, they are gifts. Sometimes we exchange works, like Chang Fee Ming's artworks, for example. So, I definitely can't sell those – they are too valuable and I can't even put a price on them.

My studio and my gallery are next to each other. I need space to work in, but I also need space to display everything that I have collected or worked on, so that they are continuously in my line of sight, as they inspire me to keep working. So, it's not a commercial space but more like an inspirational space. In Indonesia, in places like Jogja and Bali, you do see more of this concept of a studio/gallery.

Originally the reception hall and sitting room of the shophouse, now transformed into a gallery with a newly-constructed mezzanine floor for additional storage. The ceiling is intentionally left bare to expose the structural aesthetics of the original floor joists.

The original timber panelled doors, panelled ceiling, staircase handrail, and balusters were maintained and given a fresh coat of paint.

Originally a bedroom, now revamped into an open workspace and lounge on the second floor of the shophouse. The windows open out into the air well. The original timber flooring has been painted.

This particular shophouse overlooks one of my favourite places to eat, Ann Loke café. I enjoy their authentic local coffee and the ambience, which reminds one of the olden days.

CURRENT PRACTICE

One of the recurring subject matters in your illustrations and paintings is the hilt of the *keris*. Can you tell me more about your fascination with the *keris*?

I have been absorbed in portraying this unique weapon for many years and I am still in the process of learning more about the symbolism embodied in its design. Through the motifs carved on the *keris*, we can trace its origin. For example, we can identify whether the artefact comes from Langkasuka, Patani, or Indonesia.

Many people don't realise that the hilt of the *keris* is like a thumbprint, in a sense that it carries the identity of its owner. For example, if I were to travel to Ayodhya and I happen to die in combat, my companion would return home carrying my *keris* as evidence of my death. People would be able to recognise from the design of my *keris* that it belonged to me.

Part of the attraction of the *keris* is also the mystical process that goes into its making. Before you can make the hilt, you need to feel its energy and you need to have a sense that you are ready to begin. If your mind is troubled, the tools may be in front of you but you cannot enter into the process.

You are an architect by profession. What are you currently working on?

Right now, I am involved in the conservation project of the *Istana Sri Menanti* in Negeri

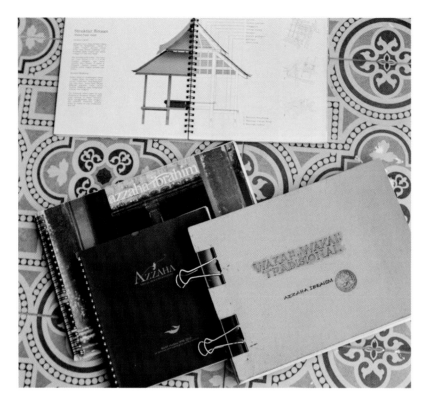

Measured drawings and information on the traditional wakaf collected over the years, which Azzaha hopes to publish one day. 1. Wakaf Langkasuka, 2012 (photos, measured drawings, write-ups) 2. Travel book entitled Azzaha Ibrahim: Drawings, Paintings, Sketches (2012) 3. Artworks 1999–2012. 4. Study on the wakaf Langkasuka 1999–2010.

Wakaf Wat Chomphrachumtat, Tumpat, Kelantan. Early 20th century. A two-tiered wakaf with a raised platform in the centre and Bumbung Perak-style roof.

Azzaha working on a painting at Wakaf Haji Latiff, Tumpat, Kelantan, which was built about 50 years ago.

AZZAHA IBRAHIM

Sembilan.[10] We are almost finishing the first phase of repairs and restoration on the main structure of the building, including the *tiang seri* (main post) which is partly damaged. If everything goes well, we will soon progress to the second phase which will make the building ready for visitors.[11]

You have also been documenting the structure of the *wakaf* in Kelantan. How did that come about?

I became obsessed with the structure of the *wakaf* about 15 years ago. People would look at it and say 'It's just a roof over four pillars with no walls, what's so special about it?' But they don't realise that it's so much more than that.

What attracted you to the *wakaf* as a structure?

The *wakaf* is built according to the height of a person. This means that it is anthropometrically designed, taking into consideration its communal functions. So, if we study the *wakaf*, we can get to know the culture and way of life of the societies who built it. They did not build it in haste, like so much of what we do now. If you look at the *wakaf*s built today, many of them are out of

proportion and also aesthetically unappealing. But the *wakaf* of old is built by artisans who care enough to design it proportionately and decorate it with meaningful motifs. This means that the design goes beyond utilitarian considerations. For example Wakaf Haji Latiff is one of the most beautiful *wakaf*s, in my opinion.

You also have a keen interest in manuscripts?

I have always been interested in old manuscripts like *Hikayat Abdullah*,[12] *Sejarah Pattani*,[13] and also another ancient text on the *keris Melayu*.[14] Whenever I visit different towns, I try to go to the libraries to see if they have interesting manuscripts. Some are also borrowed from my friends, and cover a variety of topics such as the Malay Kamasutra or *azimat* (charms).

I have been writing my own manuscript, a compilation of materials I have found that can be attributed to the old kingdom of Langkasuka. This includes the symbolism found in craft such as the carvings on weaponry, motifs on textiles, ornaments in architecture and folklore.

MATERIALS AND TOOLS

When I travel, I always bring along a small watercolour set and my sketchbooks. And I choose interesting places where people congregate, and sit down and observe. So, all I need is a simple set, nothing fancy. I can work anywhere.

I also like to work with a pencil when I'm writing my manuscript. I find the simplest tools like the pencil the best to work with. For my paintings, I use acrylics, charcoal on canvas. I've also done watercolours or ink on rice paper.

WORKING PROCESS

Can you describe your working process? How do you go about doing measured drawings?

I usually go to people's houses and tell the residents that I want to do some research on their house. They look at me suspiciously and, at first, they may not allow me inside the house, only outside.

So, I sit outside the whole day. I draw, I take measurements. I don't go for lunch. They ask me, 'Aren't you going to eat?' I say, 'It's okay... I want to finish this.'

The next day when I turn up again, I bring some fruits with me. This time, they welcome me, invite me into the house and even allow me to go into their rooms. That's when I get a chance to see the fantastic woodcarvings in the different parts of the house. I did this for about five years. I became obsessed with it [laughs]. After that, I became interested in Chinese Peranakan[15] shophouses, temples, *wakaf*, et cetera.

Were you funded in anyway?

If I waited for funding, I would end up doing nothing. I can't wait. I just do it on my own time, using my own resources. So, I have my architectural practice. This helps me.

What's your typical day like?

I wake up early in the morning and after prayers, I socialise a bit with my friends, and then I'm ready to work at about 10 a.m. I work till evening, and then, when everyone has gone back, that's when I start my own work. When the other colleagues leave the office, it's time for me to relax and do my own thing. I go to my table, switch on my lamp and there, I slowly start work on my manuscript or paintings and drawings.

Notes

1 *Wayang Kulit* is the traditional Malay art of shadow puppetry; the puppeteer is called *dalang*.

2 *Keris* is a traditional Malay dagger characterised by its unique wavy, double-edged damascene blade and pistol-grip handle.

3 *Wau* is the large Malay kite traditionally flown by the menfolk of Kelantan to celebrate a successful harvest.

4 *Batik* refers to both the traditional Malay process of printing designs on fabric using the wax-resist dyeing method, as well as to the traditional textiles produced through this technique.

5 A *wakaf* is a traditional roofed pavilion without walls and with a low, raised platform as a floor.

6 Langkasuka is an ancient Malay Hindu–Buddhist kingdom reputed to have existed in the Malay Peninsula between the 2nd–15th century AD.

7 Nik Rashiddin Haji Nik Hussein (died 2002), a renowned master of Kelantan woodcarving.

8 Akademi Nik Rashiddin is collaboratively managed by Rosnawati Othman and Nik Rashidee Nik Hussein (the wife and brother respectively of the late Nik Rashiddin), Norhaiza Noordin and Azzaha Ibrahim. Located in Bachok, it showcases the woodcarving works of the late Nik Rashiddin, and includes a collection of Malay artefacts and Malay vernacular house on stilts.

9 *Janda berhias*, which literally means 'decorated widow', is a term for decorated wall panels.

10 The *Istana Sri Menanti* (Sri Menanti Palace) in Negeri Sembilan was completed in 1908 and constructed entirely without the use of nails. Based on the precepts of traditional architecture, its posts were joined using hardwood dowels and rivets, while the *tiang seri* (main post) was sourced from a single tree trunk.

11 In 2019, the palace was reopened to the public. The conservation process has been detailed in a book titled, *Konservasi Istana Lama Seri Menanti*, by Shaari Mat Saod and Azzaha Ibrahim, Melaka: Publicious.TV, 2019.

12 *Hikayat Abdullah* is the autobiography of Abdullah Abdul Kadir, better known as Abdullah Munsyi, first published in 1849. Abdullah Munsyi was a Malay scribe who lived in Melaka and Singapore.

13 *Sejarah Pattani* (The History of Pattani) is a traditional account of the Patani empire from the 14th century to the 17th century. Patani is now part of South Thailand.

14 An early 19th century manuscript about the Malay *keris*, written by Abdul Samad Faqih Abdullah, also known as Tok Pulai Chondong, a renowned *ulama* (religious scholar/leader) of that era from Kelantan.

15 Also known as the 'Straits-born Chinese' or *Baba Nyonya*. A culturally syncretic community descended from intermarriages between Chinese immigrants who came to the Malayan Archipelago between the 15th-19th centuries C.E., and the local populace.

SHIA YIH YIING
THE ART OF INNOCENCE AND EXPERIENCE

Shia Yih Yiing is a figurative painter who works primarily with oils. She is also one of very few professional artists who has been teaching adult art classes at the Malaysian Institute of Art (MIA). As a painter, Yih Yiing is known for her powerful portraits that illustrate her own life stories using allusions from popular fiction and history. Her family members, who have served as inspiration for many of her narratives, are a recurrent theme in her work. Through her depictions of her son, two daughters and husband, she adopts the role of an acute observer and story-teller.

Her journey in art has thus become a way of finding her own voice in this world. She recalls her days of youth in Kuching when she thought life seemed to hold little meaning or purpose. However, an art scholarship awarded by MIA,[1] then one of the pioneer art institutions in Kuala Lumpur, changed her views on life. The fundamentals of observation and critical thinking through art practice shaped her worldviews and her sense of self. She noted that in the early days of her career as an artist, she depicted her dreams and hopes in her art. In this sense, her early art reflected the innocence and anticipation of starting out a new life with her own family.

However, she remarks that once she started having her own children, her outlook towards life changed. She began to look at the world through the discerning eyes of a parent whilst simultaneously expressing the innocent viewpoint of the child. For instance, in her series, *The More We Get Together*, Yih Yiing depicts her daughter dressed in different traditional attires of various ethnic communities in Malaysia. In each figure, her daughter is portrayed in stylised gestures appropriated from various European Baroque paintings of the 17th century. Her realistic portrayal of her daughter's face and the clothes she wears, are placed in an obviously fictional setting. She presents a juxtaposition of contradictory notions: a child displaying mature and dramatic gestures, the almost happy meeting of cultures implied through traditional costumes, contrasted with the serious and distant posturing of each figure against a surrealist backdrop. Yih Yiing presents these multiple oppositions as a way of commenting on the hypocrisy of the world we live in.

As an art teacher, she emphasises the importance of sustained thinking about the issues that concern us. It is only through deliberate contemplation that we may gain real insight and understanding of our life's purpose. Her art classes encourage students to share personal stories and to be narrators of their own circumstances. She states that art, after all, is about our accumulated experiences and how we choose to live.

Her techniques towards figuration and composition have been honed over the years by looking towards the great story-tellers of the Renaissance, such as Leonardo da Vinci or Sandro Botticelli, as well as masters from the Baroque period. Coming from a Roman Catholic family, Yih Yiing has long been fascinated with religious iconography. She says, 'I have always worked with visual references and found it an enjoyable approach.' Her use of familiar imagery, icons or symbols helps her create a connection between the audience and the work.

Fairy tales and children's fiction such as Lewis Carroll's *Alice in Wonderland*, have also been appropriated in her work. Such fantastic tales exemplify the contrary perspectives she often takes in narration. She portrays a world as seen through the innocent eyes of a child, filled with curiosity, faith and wonder, mixed with puzzlement and confusion. In contrast, it is through the lens of experience that she expresses her dissatisfaction and critique of the Malaysian political situation, and how it shapes our social, cultural identities and our physical environments. The health of our relationships with each other and our relationship with nature have also become subjects of interest to Yih Yiing in recent years. It has become her impetus to develop personal strategies for sustainable living and ultimately, a greater appreciation of the simple life.

Monumental Abundance (2006), a nod to her growing up years in Batu 5, Kuching, in a neighbourhood surrounded by ceramic factories.

GROWING UP

Can you remember your first exposure to art?

I grew up in an orchard in Kuching. My father was a primary school teacher. I didn't have much exciting activity, apart from playing with cousins in the orchard, climbing trees, catching fish – that kind of wild childhood. It was very memorable.

I recall having a habit of tearing out the pages of my exercise books to draw on, and I regret not keeping any of it. I think in Primary Six, I started making greeting cards with Japanese manga figures, as a Chinese New Year greeting for my classmates. I was also encouraged by my father, who sent me for art competitions, where I received some awards. So, that's how I found my way and my skills.

Did he teach you art?

No, he didn't really teach me. He just bought me oil pastels which were imported from Japan. It was quite expensive and beautiful. He just let me discover it for myself. In my secondary school years, he started buying art magazines. But I regret not really reading them as a kid. There were articles on modern art and abstract art, but I only remember being attracted to the Nanyang style, especially the works of Cheong Soo Pieng. My father did watercolour artworks during his free time, painting still life with local fruits, and I followed him.

Then, my secondary art teacher encouraged me to take up proper art lessons. In Form 1 or Form 2, I started going to watercolour classes in one of the art schools in Kuching. It was conducted by a lady artist trained in Hong Kong.

My earlier life in Kuching was extremely boring. After finishing Form Six,[2] I worked in a small office, then later in a factory. I think I was 22 when I started to think about my life and my future. I cried, you know? My mum saw it. I looked at the sky – it was a rainy day. I said, 'Am I going to be like this forever? Finished?' I felt like my soul was 30 or 40 years old already. So that's why winning the MIA (Malaysian Institute of Art) scholarship changed my life totally.

LEARNING PROCESS

Tell me about your experience at MIA

I came to MIA at the age of 23 but I treasured every moment. The training in MIA is 'American style' – it's very free. The lecturers basically don't really teach you the techniques; they just teach verbally, they don't really touch the work or demonstrate. So basically, you have to struggle; but I came in with good skills, so I had no problems. But with Chinese ink paintings, I can paint the 'skin' but I cannot paint the soul. I can produce beautiful Chinese ink paintings, but I had one of the lowest marks.

Why was that?

I didn't really follow the 'rules'. I understood it superficially on the surface level, but not its essence. So, there was a hindrance to me learning things because I thought I already had good skills. One of my lecturers said that most of the scholarship winners who came to MIA didn't do well, because their skills became a hindrance to them – they refused to learn new things. So I did struggle. I actually struggled all the way, until now.

Were you also teaching then?

I worked part-time and studied full-time. I was lucky to get a post in MIA as a children's art tutor. I worked hard on my assignments, and during the weekends, I taught. I didn't really socialise. Just studied well to get my diploma and then I met my husband. So I graduated with 2 certificates: graduation and marriage cert [laughs].

How did becoming a teacher help you in your learning process?

After I graduated, I taught kids. In fact, before coming to KL, in Kuching, I was already teaching kids in Form Six. But the kids would just come and go; so, perhaps because of that, I didn't feel a sense of achievement because there was no continuity.

Then I realised that my adult classes were different, because it was during these classes that we shared stories from people of different backgrounds, cultures, nationalities and circles. That is really important. It made me a full, whole person. It made me appreciate what I have.

I live in a small world but teaching really opened my eyes to the real world. I am curious about their lifestyles. When I hear all my students' life stories, I also share my experiences with them. I only realised the importance of my class when my students told me that it's so therapeutic. It's like recharging yourself. I never thought of that.

How do you see your work developing as a result of this?

In my earlier years, I use to paint portraits to tell stories from my worlds, my dreams – not my 'real world'. Often, they were an escape for me. In my very first self-portrait, I painted myself in a Venus pose from Botticelli, and my dream to have a garden. Then later, when I had kids, I started painting more about the big world, the 'real world'. I realise that life is a learning process of how to live as a person. I want to live in the moment. I want to practice a simple life. Now I'm living my dream. I have my own edible garden. I've been doing that for the past four years, and now, I want to translate that into my art to inspire others.

SPACE AND PLACE

Tell me about your current workspace

Actually I grew up in a big family and I've always been dreaming of having my own house. Since primary school, I've been drawing my dream house. I drew and drew and drew until I was 43 [laughs]. When we knew that we could build a house here, I drew the house plan, after much research. We knew what kind of space we wanted. I took 10 years to draw the plan for the house and to design the interior.

Where were you working before you had this space?

After I got married, I found out that my husband had an old half-abandoned house in this part of the city. There was still a family living there [as tenants], but my husband's family had moved out, so their section of the house was left empty. I asked them if I could use it as a studio. It was filled with old furniture but I painted it and rearranged it. I was working in that studio for 15 years.

This [current] house took one year to build. During that time, we moved to a shop lot in Menjalara, I think, for five to six years.

Yih Yiing started her gardening project with ferns and cacti before deciding she wanted to grow an edible garden in her backyard. She has cultivated leafy greens, beans, lime, *bunga telang* (butterfly pea flower), as well as *pucuk paku* (an edible wild fern) which is enjoyed as a popular stir-fried dish in Sarawak.

The third floor was designed to house the working spaces for the whole family with an attic for storage. Furniture on wheels are used so that Yih Yiing can move her work station around to catch the natural light.

Yih Yiing teaches adult art classes in her home cum studio. Her ex-students from MIA meet up to brainstorm for an art workshop collaboration. 'I don't see enough of the world, so there are limitations when I work alone, whereas working together allows contrasting views of the world to be presented.' Artworks: *The More We Get Together* series (2009–2013).

A bicycle against a wall with two artworks, a painting done for World Wildlife Fund, 2000s, which hangs above *Smile! Princess Smile* 2014.

Actually, my present studio is the best [I've ever had]. I have the best space and the best time, but I have the worst production [laughs].

Is it too comfortable?

I think so. Previously, I was busy, I was lost, and I wanted to do something for myself, so I didn't think too much. I just did the work. But now I have plenty of time to think, and I think too much. But maybe it's good because I have time to reflect on what I have done. I have been doing nothing much but thinking about how to live a simple life.

CURRENT PRACTICE

You're working on a series of small paintings featuring birds. Tell me more about these birds as a recurring subject matter in your work.

Birds are my fascination. When I was young, I liked to look at birds. I have a vivid childhood memory of wanting to keep a pigeon but my father let it fly away. It was pink and green and the prettiest bird I have ever seen. So, on and off in my paintings, I will paint wild pigeons. I also paint the *merbok* (zebra dove) and the *bubut* (coucal) which lays eggs in my garden. And it's amazing – it's very fast, from the time it lays its eggs to the time the babies fly off… within weeks, they are gone. I also painted the Omen Birds[3] of Borneo, [the Iban] follow the cry of these birds to go up hunting or to come back. There are 35 pieces in total.

You've added another layer of meaning to the work through your use of iconic religious figures. Can you elaborate on this?

My family is Roman Catholic. I used to see the posters of holy icons from Christianity at a young age. I don't really go to church, but there is this connection there due to this exposure. During Western colonisation, missionaries came with governors and they brought a change of life to the ordinary people in terms of education, work and how to create a livelihood. Today, religion has become like 'direct sales' – what they are selling is a service to give you peace of mind.

So, in this series, I'm using the icons metaphorically as horizons. These figures appear as landscape [features] rather than the main actors – figures like Jesus, Adam and Eve, Joseph and Mary Magdalene who wandered in the wild. I also appropriate elements from classical paintings of the Renaissance and the Baroque periods. I really enjoy copying familiar images. That is an approach which I have been using for a long time. Sometimes I also appropriate the compositions. I do this to create connections with the public. I would like the viewers to think about it and interpret it for themselves.

How are you working on developing this into a video?

The video has developed into something different from the paintings. It is the story of the land. There will be an installation to show how we have wasted the land by the ways we are consuming it. So, I did a brief history of the oil palm, when it was introduced and where and how it resulted in environmental damage.

The story begins with an image of fruits which turn into birds, they then change into burning haze. The bird changes into a rooster, and then into the mynah, which reflects its transformation from a *kampung* (village) bird into a city bird.

I work with interns from UNIMAS[4] on this project. They are familiar with animation. The stop-motion animation is very tedious work. So, the designs are mine, but they help me execute it as animation. In the process, they learn how I develop my ideas. When they have a technical problem, they just google for a solution. I really enjoy that, and I am looking forward to working with groups.

MATERIALS AND TOOLS

Where do you get your art materials?

I buy ready-made, primed canvases. I buy my oil paint in bulk. This is from Germany [Schmincke's Norma] which I bought in Penang. The oil seems to separate from the pigment – that's a problem because I buy in bulk. There is 'artist' grade and 'student' grade, so I just get the 'artist' grade. But I'm not particular about the paint. I also use Daley Rowney and recently, Windsor & Newton for acrylics.

Above, left and right: References from different books on Renaissance and Baroque paintings, and on tropical bird species.

A perspex artist's palette, a gift from a senior in college is still in use today.

Are you particular about how you use the materials?

I don't do mixed media. I use acrylic for the background for a quick start up, but I really enjoy oil because it can be manipulated well. I use the palette knife to mix colours and to spread the colours on to the canvas and to clean the brush, it's a must for me but I don't use it to paint.

I don't like to be messy, so I use only one palette, unless I am working with only one colour, in which case I use bottle caps. I use the Chinese bristle brush, because its cheap. Whenever a bookstore closes down, I buy the stock in bulk.

I am also very careful about oils because the fumes are poisonous. During my three pregnancies I used acrylic. I also tell my students not to keep washing their brushes during a painting session, as I am allergic to it. After I paint, I don't wash my hands directly because it is still warm. I wipe my hands with a tissue. If I need to eat, I use chopsticks.

WORKING PROCESS

Can you elaborate on your working process with an example?

Usually it's a series of connections. For example, the painting *Once Upon a Time* (2007), started with my youngest daughter being very interested in Barbie stories and the Barbie princesses. That is what got me fascinated with Western fairytales. It sparked off the idea of a fairy godmother whom I later turned into a fairy 'goodmother'. And I thought of the Twin Towers, because it sounded like it came from a fairytale!

Then I asked myself, 'Well, where do I stand? What is my role in all of this?' I thought, 'Why not portray myself as the Fairy Goodmother, babysitting five baby princesses who have been cursed with a deadly spell?' They all come from different kingdoms, but now they are cursed and live in the Twin Towers in the middle of the sea – Southeast Asia! Now they await the Prince Charming.

And is your subsequent painting, *Tell Us One Story*, a continuation of the story of the five princesses?

After that show, I felt like I wanted to see these princesses grow up. What would happen to them when they grow up? Well, they are playing and they are together, but they never really touch each other. It's just like our ethnic groups today. We are like islands. We say 'hi' and then we part. We don't interfere with each other's lives. But we should be like a family.

What I'm trying to say is that it's such a beautiful nation, and having different ethnic groups should teach us tolerance. It should teach us respect. It's such a good ground to practice this basic human behavior.

How many hours do you paint at a time?

It depends. Usually half a day, because painting for me is like a ritual. Once you've built the momentum, you have to go on. I must finish colouring. I force myself because I don't want to waste. I must know when the deadline is, because I don't do last minute work.

How long do you work on a piece?

It depends on how much preparation I have done with the idea and concept. Sometimes I have a rough idea, like 50% to 60%, so I will just start and, along the way, I will deal with the little things like, what kind of background and what kind of colours? If I'm not rushed, then I can take months. There are works that takes years.

I also have a thumbnail sketch with the colour scheme as well. Then, I would sleep over it and question myself, 'Is it necessary?', or 'Is there any impact and, if so, what is the impact?' Sometimes, I will double-check with my previous works and see if there's any recurrence. If there's a recurrence, I wonder, 'Should I maintain it?' Recently, I discovered a recurrence with works from 20 years back. Same colour scheme, same bird, same pose. I didn't realise it when I was painting it. It's very interesting for me to go back to what concerned me a long time ago, but to have a fresh perspective on it.

Do you have a typical day?

I enjoy my mornings. My morning starts with breakfast, coffee and reading the newspaper. Then I go to the studio and I push myself to start the painting. I usually stop sometime in the evening. I don't paint at night because I don't see the colours well when I'm tired. In the evenings, I usually prepare a simple dinner or do my gardening. The night-time is spent reading or watching a drama series or movies on TV, but mostly reading. It's a very simple life.

Can you elaborate on your teaching process?

For beginners, I teach them basic drawing and painting techniques, based on a single object, a blue ceramic jar – a much-hated subject for them [laughs].

Those who are strong-headed sometimes refuse. 'Why do I have to do this? This looks so child-like.' I usually say, 'Just do it once to experience it, and the experience will stay with you a lifetime.' I ask them to face the same subject, the same object repeatedly, so that they learn to look at it in a different way each time, and learn to develop their ideas thematically later on.

After learning the basics, I ask them to repeat the same techniques with conventional subject matter such as still life, landscapes, portraits or abstraction, focusing on compositions and content. Then I introduce them to Modern Art styles, studying the techniques of 10 figurative artists and 10

abstract artists, by studying their iconic works in still life, portraits or landscapes. For the students, this is so much fun.

I also use daily life experiences to teach, instead of artistic terms. I ask them, 'Why do you do it this way? Does it reflect what you do in real life?' This way, they find out more about themselves.

Notes

1   Malaysian Institute of Art.

2   The highest level of secondary education in Malaysian public schools.

3   The Seven Omen Birds of the indigenous Iban community in Borneo, comprise the *ketupong* (rufous piculet), *beragai* (scarlet-rumped trogon), *bejampong* (crested jay), *pangkas* (maroon woodpecker), *embuas* (banded kingfisher), *kelabu papau* (Diard's trogon) and the *nendak* (white-rumped Shama). The Iban ascribe specific customs and rituals to their daily activities, depending on the nature of one's encounter with these Omen Birds.

4   Universiti Malaysia Sarawak.

The collection of books for the whole family. The collection on the ground floor is mainly for reference and fully available to her students. It includes children's fiction, art catalogs, her husband's fine art books, and her sister-in-law's books on textile and fashion.

Left: Chinese fiction belonging to Yih Yiing's sister-in-law.

Right: Yih Yiing's husband's personal library of non-fiction literature and coffee table books.

ILSE NOOR
WONDROUS LANDSCAPES:
HISTORIES, LEGENDS AND MYTHS

Ilse Noor is known as an artist engraver, painter, poet, and writer. As a printmaker, she is renowned for her beautifully meticulous intaglio technique of etchings and aquatints. As a writer and poet, she has published many autobiographically inspired works based on her own life, as well as on her interest in the history and culture of the Malay kingdoms.

Her interest in archaeology is captured in *Warisan Nusa,*[1] a published book of etchings on Malay traditional architectures which includes palaces and houses. In the book, Ilse not only produces sensitive renderings of these dwelling places, but also offers personal accounts of her journeys and experiences. She says that the etchings of the houses are not merely historical documentation, but are really portraits. Her recognition of such abodes as 'personalities' rather than architecture reflects the notion of the abode as a living entity. She captures not only the historical representation of the house, but also expresses the intangible aspects of the building, such as the stories of its inhabitants that linger on long after their passing. Her readings on the historical sites and the people who inhabit them are weaved into her personal experience of the place, which informs the production of her drawings and etchings.

Ilse is not only interested in historical texts but is also intrigued by the possibilities of unknown stories and myths that surround historical narratives. Her interest in the historical literature of Southeast Asia is often combined with her appreciation of traditional folklore, oral histories and legends. She follows the archaeological discoveries of diverse kingdoms of the Malay world with much interest.

She muses that the traditional cultures of the Malay Archipelago are one of inimitable refinement – a culture which is very sensitive to nature and its elements. Ilse has thus developed a technique in etching that is extremely intricate and sophisticated to express these qualities.

In the art of intaglio[2] printmaking, Ilse was trained in the classical tradition of the *peintre graveur* (artist engraver), as one who designs the drawing, etches it, inks it and prints it.[2] There are very few artist engravers in Malaysia, let alone one who is classically trained. Her virtuoso use of the steel needle lends her work such precision that it reinforces the believability of her landscapes. However, her approach towards etching is surprisingly intuitive and does not at all conform to a strict adherence to rules, as one might expect of such detailed and consistent work.

Growing up in Germany where much steel was produced, her familiarity with metals like copper and steel are evident in the way she treats them. Her etching process demands a high degree of patience and the ability to visualise the final print in the mind's eye. Such elaborate work is what attracts Ilse to etching as a medium of choice. She notes that she does not find her work tiring, simply because she finds immense pleasure from working with the metal and has developed a keen sense of its behavior.

This sensitive knowledge of the materials is combined with a strong sense of graphic design – the ability to translate complex three-dimensional forms in nature into clearly articulated linear drawings. Her development in art has also been impacted by the Vienna School of Fantastic Realism. While outwardly, the approaches of Fantastic Realism may appear similar to those of the Surrealists, the proponents of the former did not rely on actual dreams or the subconscious as direct subject matters for their works. Rather, they combined mystical symbolism with actual forms in nature to rationally develop their work. While the landscapes they depict are metaphysical, they emerge from an intellectual response to both the fictive and the real, rather than from a subconscious state.

Ilse's works are great examples of such an approach. Through her own research and observations, she ventures beyond the physical appearance of nature. Her art practice has led her into a world of wonder where reality meets fantasy. It is powerful and it draws us into a space where the potentialities of a spiritual or metaphysical dimension are emphasised. Through her work, we are persuaded to consider such possibilities and to acknowledge its presence in our physical and current worlds.

GROWING UP

Can you recall your earliest exposures to art?

I was born in '41 during the war. We had no paper, we had no pencil, no coloured pencils – nothing. So we were hungry for materials. When I went to school, we had a small blackboard made of slate. When you did your homework, after showing it to the teacher, you had to wipe it with a sponge and start again. So all the information had to be in your head. What you learned in school was memorised and not written in books. So, you were trained to observe, you were trained to remember and to work with something like the etching needle that's sharp, which you will have to remove later on.

Today, they can paint with watercolours and they have all kinds of things. But my world, then, was very muted? I must admit that I can't look at strong colours. It gives me a migraine… strong orange, yellow or green [laughs]. Later we got exercise books and we were taught to write with nib and ink to develop our cursive writing (which is technically similar to calligraphy). That was a different time when small things made your life happy and you learned to be contented with your materials.

Have you always wanted to study art?

No, I thought I wanted to study archaeology because I had books on adventures and archaeological excavations, and there were all these drawings inside that were excellent. So it was more the idea of going to places and looking at old things and drawing them. I just wanted to draw those things. I don't think I really wanted to study archaeology! I read adventure books, like the original Tarzan books or 'World without the White People', and I read about these faraway countries and I was obsessed with it. But for example, if I wanted to study archaeology I had to learn Greek. I said, 'No, no, I don't want to do that. I just want to draw.' So my mother (my father had died in WWII) allowed me to go for private art classes. I enjoyed that so much.

I had a good teacher, Willy Maria Stucke. A portrait artist, very classical. I was 16 at that time but I never heard of the word 'artist', we call it *künstler*.

Then, I did a practicum at a graphic company but I did not want to stay there. So, my mother said, 'Go visit your uncle in Cologne.' He was a graphic artist (as I learned later on) for 'commercial graphic'. My uncle advised me to go to the Kölner Werkschule. The concept of the Kölner Werkschule followed the same concept as the famous Bauhaus school, but due to World War II, there was not enough teaching staff or artists anymore. So, when Kölner Werkchule restarted again, it functioned more as an institution to elevate and refine the skills and tastes of gifted craftsmen and artisans, to enable them to reach a higher level in their profession. It was good but I did not feel challenged, so I applied to the Academy of Fine Arts in Munich.

A wooden crafted pencil case from her school days, still in use today to house her tools.

Ilse's children's book based on her childhood in Hückeswagen, Germany. Books published (clockwise): *Das alte Haus auf Hartkopsbever* (The Old House on the Hill) (1970), *Cenderawasih: The Seven Dreams, The Seven Places* (1989), *Ludwigs Baum- Bilderbuch* (1982), *Warisan Nusa: Shell Book of Malaysian Heritage* (1991). On the right is a blackboard from her schooldays.

LEARNING PROCESS

When did you start learning printmaking?

At the Academy of Fine Arts, you had to select the professor under whom you wanted to study. By then, with my private teacher, I had already done graphic arts and I liked it so much. So I selected my professor who was teaching Sacral Painting and Fine Art Graphic. There were 200 applicants for him and there was only a limited space available for study. He took five boys and one girl – that was me.

Can you describe your experience studying under him?

He was a good arts teacher but it was very difficult. We all worked very hard but they never forced us. You are not controlled, you are not asked to do this or that. But the whole class was very intense. You stand your easel next to each other and work, work, work... I could see the power of their work. Sometimes you can only hear the scribbling of the brush on canvas and sometimes a boy would play classical guitar. It was very stimulating and you are carried away by this whole working atmosphere.

In printmaking too, they don't tell you what you must do and how to do it and which way to do it. You make mistakes and you learn from others when you watch them, but there's no one correct way in that sense, in terms of technique. They only tell you what to buy and I bought them, and since then, I've grown to like these materials and have stuck to them.

So, in that sense, you have developed your own process for printmaking?

I have a very classical idea of printmaking. But yes, I have to experiment with it and get a feel for it. You can't depend on rules for printmaking. For example, I've worked with acid for a long time. The acid determines the intensity of the shadows... And when you put your plate into the acid, you need to know how long to leave it in the acid bath and I rely on my feel for it, whether it's a few seconds or a minute. It's different when the humidity in the air is different, or when there is a storm. You have to play with the acid to know how it will behave.

Were you influenced by Rembrandt at all when you were a student?

Well, yes. Rembrandt and Francisco de Goya as well. But not in the sense that I was influenced by his technique, because Rembrandt's graphical work is executed in passionate dramatic lines, creating a painterly effect (similar to his oil paintings) until the etchings appear very dark, almost black. This effect may be caused by different acids he used besides the Dutch bath, like iron ferric or sulphur and different types of metal plates.

This is not suitable for my work. I was more interested in Ernst Fuchs who was a Vienna Surrealist artist. Technique wise, Fuchs is what intrigues me because he produced very beautiful works which are very fine. If I used Rembrandt's lines, I would not be able to capture the finer aspects that I find in the arts and culture of this region.

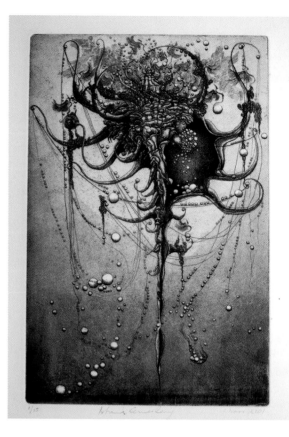

Ketibaan Puteri Sri Bunian, 2000, 13/XV.

Some of the seashells she picked up from her walks along the beach in Port Dickson. Ilse says that she has never lived near the sea and is in fact terrified of the ocean, but the arcane beauty of these tiny shells have been her inspiration for many artworks.

Right: *Istana Cemerlang*, (2001, 1/18).

SPACE AND PLACE

What are important considerations for you in terms of working space?

I don't need a big space. Since I work on a very restricted plate, the plate will determine the size of paper, and this is determined by the size of the machine.

I have a small desk where I do all my drawings. But I need an open space because the vapour from the acid is dangerous.

Do you like the landscape here in Malaysia and is this why you chose to move to the countryside?

Difficult to say, because it's different. You don't have the tones that we have (in Germany), like the black and white of winter. So, I have to use different colours, like sepia and sanguine or green-blue (permanent viridian lake) for the sea.

What do I like about the landscape here? It's very difficult to say. In the morning, you can see the mist coming up and the sun coming from the top, and it's gold and green. These are beautiful, fine colours and then in the afternoon, the sun is going down and the trees have depth, the shadows get longer and the green becomes very intense. The landscape turns into an illuminated theatre stage. And then, of course, with old architecture such as Borobudur or Prambanan, or the old wooden houses, architecture seems to melt together with nature. That is what you don't have in Europe. Buildings there are normally sitting on the surface, separated from the landscape.

Can you describe what attracts you to the culture here?

I also appreciate that the culture here is of a very different kind to the European one. I find it very refined and spiritual, having a different sort of balance. European culture on the other hand, likes a more dynamic opposition.

The spiritual culture here is very close to the water, the sea, the elements. What is interesting, too, is that there is less fear of the jungle or nature, because for the Orang Asli or the Malays… the jungle is their protection. For example, in Indonesia people live near the volcano – it's very dramatic if you think about it, but that is part of their lives.

CURRENT PRACTICE

What are you currently working on?

I've been working on some etchings and writing for a book for the past two years now. It includes some anthropological essays and some old sketches from '85 which were not previously published when I worked on the *Warisan Nusa* book. For example, sketches of the Istana Kenangan in Perak and of the house in Kampung Merbok, Kedah, which belonged to the museum director in Bujang Valley; I was invited to lunch at his house.

So, I've been working on this for two years; it is also being translated from English to Malay and German, because I'm getting it ready for an exhibition in Germany.

What kinds of subject matter interests you?

I like landscapes, nature. I also love reading about the history of this place which is part of the Malay Archipelago. There is such a rich culture and an exchange of spirituality and trade, because a long time ago people could travel from island to island without the restrictions that we have today. I love reading about historical events and places that are not well-known, for example the Acehnese kingdom, Malacca, Langkasuka or Pattani.

You produced a well-known series of work on seashells. Can you tell me how that work came about?

The idea came actually from UNESCO. They asked for a scene of the sea because of the environment – that was the theme of UNESCO at the time. So I was in a group show, together with Malaysian artists Sharifah Fatimah Zubir, Juhari Said and Ismail Latiff. We were all members of this group, Ariane Essor in France.

So, in the first show, I started on the *udang* (prawn); first the fish, then the *udang*. I did a whole series on it and then gradually all this came to my mind, of this representative of the Malays as seafarers, this *lanun-lanun* (pirates)... and then my husband said, 'You must not make just one *udang*. They come in packs, these pirates.' He's always critiquing and giving me good ideas. So I did this – seven etchings on prawns – one was a *puteri* (princess), the other one was a *bidan* (midwife) and [another] a *laksamana* (admiral). So it was really interesting, yeah. So once you start, the rest automatically comes.

Are these based on a particular culture?

Not one but many. I saw in the shells, the shapes of pagodas and headdresses of dancers, not just of Malaysia, but the whole of Southeast Asia. In architecture also you'll find the forms of seashells, which has nothing to do with Buddhism or Islam, for example, you can find the pagoda form in nature everywhere. Architecture is very close to nature, its forms grow out of nature.

I also started thinking about the background of these people here, the seafarers of the archipelago who share certain similarities in languages, songs, melodies.

It reminds me very much of the atonal music in Chinese traditional opera. It is the singing of the spirits of the wind, of the sea, of the water. It is the voice of the spirits, the

Her press which is situated one level below her drawing studio, opens out into the garden.

A desk for preparing the plates. On the right is a small desk for rolling ink. On the shelf against the wall are papers stacked up in specially made boxes.

spirits' culture itself. It's connected to the sea. Sometimes I think I can hear the creaking of ropes and sails, the noise and the voices of the sea… So this is what I find beautiful. This is nature or the essence of nature.

MATERIALS AND TOOLS

Where do you buy your basic materials like the etching needles and the plates?

I use only three types of needles. These etching needles I got from Sharifah Fatimah Zubir, who bought it when she was in New York. But they are made in Germany. The metal is very pure and it comes from the ground from the area where my family lived. It is also an area where papers are made, because of the rivers and streams running through it. The water is very clean and good for paper making.

I love metal, it is a very interesting element. I like the smell of it and working with it. You cannot force the metal to do what you want to do. They have their own minds. When you are working on a plate, sometimes the line doesn't go smoothly…it resists. The metal is sulking!

I bought these plates from England; These were the best quality plates because they were hammered first to achieve a very great density, so you could get about 100 editions. You could get more, but in places like the Louvre for instance, the lifespan of a plate is about 75. They won't accept anything more than 75 editions. But if you steel-face[4] the plate, then you could get about 250 editions.

What about your papers?

The Hahnemühle paper is specially made for printing, it has been in use for the past 500 to 600 years. And it is used only for this purpose, it's not for watercolour. The French have used it for 600 years, and Germany for about 500 years. You can see where it's been made by looking for the watermark of the cockerel. This is because King George III at that time wanted to have this paper in England, and he was German. So the name Hahnemhle became well-known. *Hahne* means rooster and *mühle* is mill.

When you use good paper you can soak it 2 days in advance. They are acid-free and very lasting. They are sometimes handmade, so expensive and they come in standard sizes. They have a deckled edge and this is what the collector looks for, so it is important to not cut the paper.

When did you buy this printing press?

I had a smaller machine before this, but it was too small for the project I had to do. So I bought this machine in 1984 at the timewhen the Deutschmark was low against the Ringgit. So, this machine cost me RM8,000 together with the inks. I think now the machine would cost almost RM30,000. As for the felts, I also got these from Sharifah Fatimah Zubir, who bought it when she was in New York. It is 50 years old and still good, first class quality.

WORKING PROCESS

You have chosen etching as your printmaking technique. Can you tell me more about it?

During the old days, this technique was used to create designs on the armour plates. They would wax the plates, remove the wax with a needle, then expose the metal to acid. The acid would bite into the metal, and incise the design on to the metal. But for me, the paper is the final product. I ink the plate to transfer the image onto paper.

So I have to think in reverse, to get the mirror image of the design.

Can you describe your etching process?

Before I start on my etchings,[5] I have to prepare the metal plate, the wax, the transfer of the drawing to the waxed plate, the mordant, the ink, the printing paper and the printing press.

The metal plate needs to be cleaned until it is dust free and has no oil on it. The edges need to be beveled with a file.

Etching needles, the sharpened point for incisions, the blunt end for 'erasing' mistakes.
EMELIA ONG

Etching ball grounds from France. There are 2 types of wax; hard and soft, Ilse prefers the hard wax.

The wax I use is from France and is hard ground. The wax must not be too soft and not too hard that it cracks and splinters off when worked on.

So I use an electric plate to warm the copperplate. I've been using this electric plate for years, it's very convenient. The wax needs to melted to be dabbed on and distributed evenly, not leaving any open space. If the plate is too hot, the wax starts to steam, and I have to switch the electricity off.

How do you transfer the drawing to the plate?

To transfer of the drawing to the waxed plate– First I have the drawing on paper. With my pencil, I trace only the outlines of the drawing onto transparent paper. I turn the transparent paper over and add a blue or black carbon paper between the transparent paper and the waxed copperplate. Through the transparent paper, the reversed image can be seen.

Then, for a second time, I redraw the outlines of the image, which will be automatically transferred as black or blue lines from the carbon paper onto the waxed metal plate.

I remove all the papers and my etching needle follows for the third time the black or blue outlines which the carbon paper had left on the waxed plate.

At this point, the work on the etching finally begins on the reversed image of the original drawing. The sharp etching needle removes the wax and exposes the hair-fine glittering lines of the metal.

Correction is not possible, so I work very slowly. I must be careful not to waste material. Once the design has been incised, it will be dipped into an acid bath. The acid will bite into the parts that are not covered by the wax. I dip it in for about six minutes, while the lighter shades only take about two to three minutes.

How do you prepare the mordant?

The mordant I use is called 'Dutch bath' or 'Dutch mordant' and it is composed of one litre of water, 30g potassium dissolved and200ml hydrochlorid acid. It is called Dutch bath because Rembrandt (master Dutch painter and printmaker) used it.

I also mix the stop-out varnish myself–I use bitumen powder dissolved in good quality

thinner. This stop-out varnish is used to cover what I don't want to expose to the acid. This process needs to be timed accurately to produce the gradual shading of different tones.

Once I've completed this process, I wash the acid off with water and remove all the wax with thinner until the plate is shining clean ready for print proofing.

Once the plate is cleaned, I apply the etching ink with a roller onto the plate.

I prefer to use the French etching ink called 'Charbonnel' which is soft, thrifty and easy to use. The colours do not fade easily.

I can use a gauze to rub the ink into the grooves and lines. I usually use the palm of my hand to rub off ink on the whole plate. But you can't do that if you are producing many plates, because your palm would start to get rough and you might transfer that

Clockwise:

A skill which Ilse has honed over the years, is the ability to write in reverse and visualize the mirror image of her designs.

Incising the design with the help of a magnifying glass

Ilse cleaning the copperplate over an electric plate.

Melting wax over the copperplate.

The dabber pushes the wax evenly over the surface of the copperplate.

The roller press comprises of two rollers with a flatbed sandwiched in between. After putting the plate onto the paper, Ilse covers it with wool felt etching blankets, consisting of the sizing catcher, the cushion and the pusher (bottom to top). The felt is a buffer that absorbs the wetness of paper and allows the ink to reach the incisions. Ilse explains that the first print is a trial proof (test) because the pressure may not be right.

Charbonnel sepia ink, an oil based ink made solely for intaglio printing.

Rubbing the inked plate to make sure the ink fills the incisions.

Buckets of different sizes are used to soak papers of different sizes evenly.

texture of your palm onto the ink! After this, I clean the edges of the plate with a cloth.

I use Hahnemühle paper and I have a collection of it. I prepare it by soaking it in water for about two hours. The paper must be wet before the ink can stick to it. And you have to be very, very clean to do this yourself, that you don't dirty the paper with your dirty fingers. You don't clean the plate and then go take another wet paper, it will immediately suck up any dirt on the plate. So I use aluminium clips to pick them up.

I clean the press with thinner and adjust the press to make sure it is tight. The machine presses the soft wet paper onto the plate. If you don't have ink on the plate, then it comes out white and blind. There are artists who do this. You will see only the impression of the etching lines (embossed).

This is my workstation, we call it a *schlitten* which means a sledge [in German]. So, you see, I'm a printmaker also (which is not the case for most artists). Previously, artists send their plates to the workshops for printing. However, nowadays in classical printmaking exhibitions, in biennales or triennales, they insist that the artist must also print their works.

Once printed, the paper comes out still wet, they have to be dried between special drying boards. They also come in different sizes. You can put them on the floor and press them down with some weight and they dry flat. You can change the boards every half hour.

How many prints would you produce in a day?

If I can produce four to five small prints in one hour, that would be good. When I was working on the *Warisan Nusa* book, I had 4 people helping me and each of us produced 20 to 30 prints a day.

I can go for about 10 hours at a time. I enjoy the process and I feel happy when I'm doing the work, so I don't feel tired.

How long do you work on a single plate?

Usually one or two months, but there are some plates that are still in progress for more than seven years! For me it is not difficult to work over a plate and improve it as I go along, I go slowly improving it. I still take it out to work with it and keep it away when I'm done for the day.

Notes

1 Ilse Noor and Adibah Amin, *Warisan Nusa*: *Shell Book of Malaysian Heritage*, Kuala Lumpur: Pustaka Cipta (1991).

2 Intaglio is an Italian term which refers to the process of printmaking where the image is produced by incision onto a surface. The image is then printed from the recessed areas of the surface as opposed to a relief print.

3 It is quite a common practice for artists to send their finished plates to a professional printer, instead of handling the printing process themselves

4 A process whereby a fine layer of iron is coated onto the surface of the copperplate through electroplating.

5 There are generally two types of etching methods: wet and dry. The former is a chemical-based technique which uses acid to make incisions onto the metal plates, while the latter uses an etching needle to incise directly onto the metal plate.

The drawing is clearly revealed once the ink has been carefully rubbed in. Tonal values in the background were created by rubbing the ink off.

The final print of the 'udang'.

PANGROK SULAP
GRASSROOTS ETHOS OF PUNK

Based in the Ranau district of Sabah, Pangrok Sulap is an art collective well known for their large-scale woodcut prints and passion for punk rock music. What began as a volunteer initiative by three friends, Rizo, Jerome and Gindung in the beginning of 2010, soon transformed into a collective as new members joined in. Together, they traversed the interiors of Sabah, carrying out activities such as printing posters, painting murals, building hydroelectric generators and screening movies, all in the spirit of creative volunteerism.

Starting out with absolutely no resources and scraping together leftover materials to create posters, Jerome recalls using waste newspaper ink for their early prints, which were then plastered onto coffee shop walls. Progressing from the naively simplistic practice of those early days, they have since developed a way of working that allows them to be financially independent. Artworks that have been produced via the medium of woodcuts are then adapted for the design of merchandise such as T-shirts, patches, bags or stickers. Part of the profits from the sale of such merchandise goes back to the community, while the remainder is used to fund the works of the collective.

Pangrok is driven by their commitment to voice the struggles of the Sabahan peoples, particularly those who are politically marginalised. All members share the same desire for community work combined with the punk attitude of protest for social justice. Through the medium of woodcut print, they work with such communities to create effective channels by which to vent their frustration and promote a wider public awareness of their grievances. With Pangrok's involvement, villagers learn the skills of woodcut artistry, and are thus empowered to speak for themselves through that medium. The banners, posters and T-shirts that the villagers create are then disseminated by the collective, who also engage the use of social media as part of the 'art process'. This approach towards art activism has created a heightened awareness of the socio-political concerns that are faced by the local communities, particularly amongst audiences outside of Sabah, through the use of social media.

Pangrok also advocates the principles of DIY (do-it-yourself) which adopts the practice of 'self-sustainability' as a way of life and rejects consumerist habits. Looking towards life in the *kampung* (village) as the ideal precedent for sustainable living, the collective adopts the motto *'Jangan Beli, Bikin Sendiri'* (Don't Buy, Do It Yourself).

As part of the grassroots community, the collective also understands their most pressing issues and helps them express complex problems, using simple yet salient messages. One poster quips: *Sinalau Bakas is cheaper than climbing Mount Kinabalu.* Pangrok explains, *Sinalau Bakas* (smoked

Left to right, top row: Rizo, Memet, Gindung; bottom row, Jerome, Jib, Bam.

wild boar) is an indigenous delicacy enjoyed by the locals. Mount Kinabalu too, is a culturally significant[1] landmark to the locals. But today the financial cost of climbing the mountain has increased to such an extent that local residents can no longer afford to experience the full beauty of their own land. The poster creates an immediate awareness of the marginalisation of the local community, caused by the privatisation (and commercialisation) of Kinabalu Park. These and other dire issues plaguing Sabah, such as illegal logging, negotiating customary land rights, sustaining traditional trades and crafts, or demanding equal access to citizenship, are highlighted through the powerful imagery of woodcut prints.

Steered by punk's anarchist underpinnings, Pangrok works as a leaderless collective. Each member is free to switch roles and take on multiple tasks independently. This approach to work avoids a hierarchical system of support and thus encourages each member to be their own leader and drive their own creative projects. As the Pangrok philosophy goes: the more people you know, the more you will learn. Each member brings something new to the table. Prior to the founding of Pangrok, Rizo was a civil engineer, Memet a graphic design graduate, Bam a psychology major, Jerome

a park ranger, while other members include henna artists, tattoo artists, zine writers, artisans and researchers. Inspired by the underground punk scene in Indonesia, they all find common ground in their collective identification with punk's radical attitudes in confronting corruption and oppression.

As the collective grew, they also discovered that producing art together with music serves to bring the members closer to one another. Pangrok members will eat, work and travel together – and this, they claim, is what keeps their fuel burning to fight the good fight. Most of the time, protest work calls for alternative strategies and creative problem-solving. This means they often have to face apathy, cynicism, censorship and criticism, as part of their efforts. There are no easy paths, but Pangrok is bent on carving out their own brand of punk, driven first and foremost, by their devotion towards empowering the forgotten communities of Sabah.

GROWING UP AS A COLLECTIVE

Tell me how you first began.

Memet: We started coming together around the end of 2009. At that time we had an infoshop called Omegashop. We sold T-shirts, art and stuff.

Rizo: There were a lot of youth that were just

hanging around outside our shop on the streets. All they did was *lepak* (loiter), drink and get drunk. So, we thought, 'Let's rope them in to try something new, like graffiti, stencilling or T-shirt printing.' For the youth, it's necessary for them to see immediate results. Once they saw that they could produce something with their own hands, they were like, '*Wah… best pulak*' (this is great), and they got excited. After that, we roped them in to do charity work under the name 'V for Volunteers'. I think it's important for people to know that punks are not just 'good-for-nothing'.

So the collective basically started as a community volunteer group? What kinds of work did you do?

Jerome: Well, it's not like we had a proper platform to do charity work. We were just friends who got together.

Rizo: Yeah, we were proactive. Hyperactive, actually [laughs]. We went everywhere and anywhere uninvited… We went to schools in rural areas, asked for permission to paint murals, collected used clothes and brought it to the remote villages, did movie screenings in the villages.

How did you all find each other?

Jerome: We are all connected by our interest in punk music. We like the lyrics, the beat, and the message it contains.

Bam: Yeah, we met through the underground music scene and continue to meet new people through these links. We go for gigs and play in different bands. Usually when there is an event, music is a big part of it. In KK (Kota Kinabalu), we had a small house for the collective so that whenever we had a gig or a music fest, friends who came from outside KK, like from Sandakan or Tawau, could just stay with us. They don't need to rent a hotel.

We collected many zines. So those who stayed in this house can read, study or make art besides attending gigs and punk rock music festivals.

So the name Pangrok Sulap was born?

Bam: Yeah, we chose '*Pangrok*' because of our passion for 'punk rock' and also because the scene emphasised the D.I.Y or do-it-yourself concept; also related to that, is the idea of fighting for one's basic human rights. *Sulap*

The beginnings of Pangrok Sulap. Standing left to right, Bam, Gindung, Gadie, Kim, Ronny, Agus. Front row, left to right, Rizo, Award, Ladem, Rambo.

RIZO

refers to the farmer's hut in the rice fields [in the Kadazandusun language]. We are all from various villages, so we felt connected to the village folk and were championing similar causes. The word *sulap* became synonymous to all of us. So *pangrok sulap* means 'punk rock hut'

Incidentally, *sulap* also means 'magic' in Bahasa Indonesia, and many Indonesians asked us what kind of magic we performed [laughs]. Each place has their own version of *sulap*: in Sarawak, it's *lepau* ('farm-hut' or 'home' in the Kayan language) and in KL, it's *pondok* ('hut' in Malay), so it's great.

Jerome: The idea of *sulap* is also related to the farmer who grows rice not just to feed himself but also to feed others. The underlying idea is that, whatever we have, whether it's a skill or knowledge, we should share it with others. When you say '*sulap*', people know you are Sabahan.

Bam: And people who live in the *kampung* don't need to buy food from outside as they grow all sorts of food themselves. They even make their own bags. So, we learn from them and DIY has become our motto.

Tell me more about the kinds of music you play.

Bam: We play Sabahan folk songs, songs by Marjinal[2] and also our own songs. Punk rock is a bit heavy and hard for most people to accept. But Sabahan folk songs such as *lagu anak kampung* (songs of the villagers) – these are easy to identify with because they speak of life in the *kampung*, common struggles of making a living and surviving. We play Marjinal songs like those that protest

corruption, *et cetera*. Rizo writes a lot of our own songs and we sing together. Basically, the message we want to send out is that our solidarity is not based on race, class, and religion; it is based on our humanity.

How did you learn the woodcut technique?

Bam: We knew a punk rock band from Japan called Vivisick. They were friends with Marjinal and they connected us with two members of the band, Mike and Bobby. One year later (in 2012), Marjinal came to tour in Peninsular Malaysia and Sabah. When they came to Ranau, we took the opportunity to learn woodcut from them.

Jerome: They had a woodcut collective called *Taring Babi* (Boar Tusks).[3]

Memet: At that time, we were already producing woodcut prints but they were not as well-crafted.

You were familiar with their prints before they came?

Bam: Yeah, there were two collectives. We were really inspired by *Taring Padi*[4] (Paddy Tusks), actually. But we learnt the methods and materials from *Taring Babi*.

Jerome: There were many collectives from Indonesia that inspired us. We used woodcut to highlight issues faced by the marginalized communities, especially in Ranau itself.

When you first started, where did you put up the posters?

Jerome: Anywhere. On walls. In coffeeshops. I suppose it was vandalism.

Rizo: Because we didn't ask for permission. But it was the truth.

Bam: It was effective. At that time hawkers who were elderly grandmothers selling *sigup* (local rollies) by the roadside were barred by the authorities from selling there.

Jerome: But then there were other vendors who were allowed to sell cigarettes in the same area. So, we asked, 'Who allowed these people to sell? How come only the local vendors were barred from selling?' So our posters made an impact because people became aware that it was a serious issue. After that, we stopped seeing these other vendors.[5]

LEARNING PROCESS

Can you recall some of the big lessons you have learnt as a collective?

Rizo: When we first started, I guess you could say we were rebels. But gradually we learned to be more positive and be an inspiration to others.

Whenever we visited the villages, we asked the people why they were unable to mobilise their youths through a collective or group. They all pointed to a lack of funding, which is given [by the government] only if you register with the ROS (Registry of Societies). But overdependence on the government will hinder us from doing something ourselves. We keep going forward, whether we get what we want or not. We always stay hopeful and relaxed.

Also, we were driven by a love for our own people and we went to these *kawasan pendalaman* (interior villages) because we came from villages ourselves. When we received a positive response from these folks, it inspired us to continue doing it. We loved to meet new people but [at that time] nobody

knew who we were, so we basically gate-crashed every event and festival [laughs].

What kind of events?

Rizo: Pesta Nelayan (Fisherman Festival) in Menumbok, *Pesta Kubis* (Cabbage Festival) in Kundasang, *Pesta Jagung* (Corn festival), *Pesta Durian* (Durian festival), *Pesta Bunga Kinabalu* (Kinabalu Flower Festival). And each time, we try to bring a message that is relevant to the local community.

For example, in *Pesta Nelayan*, we produced a woodcut print called *Laut adalah Kehidupan* (The Sea is Our Life) When they saw it, they were like, 'Yes that is true, the sea is the place we earn our living.' Only then, did they take notice of us and our work. So we kept making connections through these events and in the *tamu* (traditional indigenous market).

What are some of the major changes you have experienced as a collective?

Jerome: I think one of the major changes is the way we think about what we are doing. In the beginning, we did it without much further thought about the impact it would have on others. But now, when we do something, we realise that we need to think more broadly. It should be done for the greater good, rather than to benefit just one party.

Individually, I also feel that many of us have started to define our own purpose. Before this, a lot of us didn't really know what we wanted to do in life, so there was a lot of time wasted. But now, most of us have a better sense of our own direction.

We also learned how to manage our finances better. How to price our works better. And how to pitch and do proposals for grants.

SPACE AND PLACE

Tell me briefly about the spaces you used to have before moving to this shoplot?

Memet: When we first started in Pekan Ranau, our infoshop was very small. That was the first meeting place. We also had a house where we stayed in and our friends and visitors could also stay [referring to the studio-cum-gallery space in Ranau, at the time of the interview].[6]

Bam: The house was also a studio space to hold workshops, make art together, and print T-shirts.

Rizo: It was like a headquarters for the collective. But we couldn't use that place for the long term, because it didn't belong to us. So now we are renting this space in Ranau.

What were some of your requirements for the space?

Rizo: We already planned the space before moving here. We arranged it in such a way that we would have a space to relax and have our meetings. This is also where we sell the merchandise; then a separate space for doing silkscreen printing, a space for storage at the back and sort of a more formal space which we use as a gallery.

What are your plans for the future?

Rizo: We have plans to buy a piece of land. Because it is difficult to sustain a rented property. If we have our own land, we can build a house and do our own farming. Not only can we eat what we plant, but we can also earn a living from the sale of crops. So that would be the best for the community.

Painting the medium-density fibreboard (MDF) before drawing and carving on it.

Pangrok Sulap Merchandise: carrying the 'Tentang Ukir' brand and, on the right, their DIY motto 'Jangan Beli, Bikin Sendiri'.

Artworks produced via the woodcut medium are then used to design various merchandise. Left, 'Kami Bekerja Kerana Kami Berhutang' ('We Work Because We Are in Debt'), expressing the typical predicament of the urban worker – working hard but still drowning in debt from unpaid education loans, car loans and housing loans.

Right: Bam sewing up the patches.

CURRENT PRACTICE

Are you all doing this full-time?

Memet: No, we all have our full-time jobs. We each have our own direction in terms of selling different brands and merchandise. That's one of our targets – that individually, all of us can be financially independent.

Tell me briefly about the different brands or projects each of you are working on

Rizo: One of our (Memet and Rizo) brands is called *Tentang Ukir* (About Woodcut) which has a double meaning – '*tentang*' means 'about' in Malay, but it also means 'to oppose' or 'protest'. So it's 'about woodcut', at the same time it is also 'protest woodcut' art.

Bam: As for me, I have a shop called Artrium, which I share with a few friends. One of our brands is called *Qull*, which means 'say/speak' in Arabic. We basically print quotes, messages or sayings on T-shirts. My friend also collaborates with artists from KL and prints their designs on T-shirts.

Jerome: I'm working on a D.I.Y. toolkit for woodcut printing that is catered towards both students and artists, which comes with step-by-step instructions on making your own woodcut prints. It includes the history of woodcuts in Malaysia and Sabah. I received a grant for this.

What projects are you currently working on as a collective?

Rizo: Right now we are working on a woodcut for an event [Damai Music Sunset Festival] at Labuan. We were commissioned to do a piece which is themed 'Peace'. At the moment, we are preparing the artwork so that we can print it together as a community during the event in Labuan.

Jerome: Right now, we're also working on recycling these patches. We buy second-hand pants in bundles for a ringgit each and recycle it for printing. Pockets of various sizes are designed to be easily sewn onto bags. We also make clothes, posters, numerous merchandises like keychains, et cetera. We, ourselves, wear most of these; the idea is to be self-sustaining.

A large part of the collective's work also involves teaching others how to produce their own prints as a way to speak their mind. Tell me about this effort. Who do you teach? What is their response?

Rizo: We found that woodcut is easy to teach and it is the easiest way to spread a message. You don't need much materials to begin. We started by teaching *kampung* folk how to use woodcut to voice their problems. But we don't set any boundaries for our projects.

We do workshops with youth, veterans, kids – some as young as five years old – or even ministers, if they invite us. We want to enter every space made available to us. As long as there is an opportunity to share, we will do it.

Jerome: The results have been good. They are able to produce a print and be proud of it. The end result of an artwork depends entirely on the artist [not on us].

Just recently in 2017, your work '*Sabah Tanah Air-ku*' (Sabah My Homeland) was taken down from the 'ESCAPE from the SEA' exhibition in Kuala Lumpur because it was deemed 'too sensitive'.[7] Can you recall your thoughts during that time?

Jerome: I think that people need to look at our work from a larger perspective and realise that a lot of what we are dealing with is not just happening in Malaysia. They are global issues.

Everywhere you go, there is the good and the bad side of things. There is no escaping it. That was part of our concept for the show. That was why we had two corresponding pieces of work. But some people had the wrong idea that we were anti-government because they understood it from a limited point of view. But it's ok. It's good to talk about these things.

Has that affected the collective in any way?

Rizo: Actually we are quite curious to know what other people think about it [laughs]. It was not really a big deal. We still continue to do the same things we did when we started.

In 2014 you exhibited for the first time in Tokyo, how has this experience shaped your work here?

Jerome: Our friend [Risa Tokunaga] from Japan, is a lecturer and writer in Tokyo [at the Tokyo University of Foreign Studies], and she shared our work there [at the Irregular Rhythm Asylum]. The impact of the [woodcut] collective in Japan is huge. This created awareness about the Kaiduan Dam overseas.[8] I think more Malaysians knew about the dam only after the news went to Japan because the local media did not publicise it, even though it was so strongly protested. But after the Japanese news media covered it, it received more attention in local media. The last I heard, they stopped their plans to build the dam.

Rizo: Some people say we are an 'international' collective because we have exhibited overseas in Japan. But nothing's changed…

Memet: We are still… *orang kampung* (village folk).

Jerome: Yeah, we still feel the same about doing this type of work. This is what we like to do.

Memet: We still want to go to the *kampung* to do volunteer work.

Rizo: Yeah, that has not changed. Even till today, we still love going back to the villages and helping out whenever we can. *Kami orang kampung!* (We are village folk!) It is our source of knowledge.

What are some of the most memorable places you have visited?

Jerome: There're too many. We've been to Johor, Selangor, KL, Kedah, Seberang Perai, Tioman and others. In Sabah, we've been to so many places like Narawang, Lutut, Pakolen, Tambunan. I think one of the best experiences was in Kampung Buayan.[9]

Bam: Yeah, it was the best. There was no line, no internet connection, so you couldn't use the phone – you're completely cut off from the world. But we had the best time there.

Jerome: We gained knowledge about herbs.

Rizo: Knowledge about the jungle

Jerome: It was a new experience, even though we already knew our way around the jungle.

Bam: You forget everything… You go look for *sayur hutan* (edible plants) in the jungle.

Rizo: They teach us everything – the best places to look for fish, how they grow their crops. Basically they shared with us their daily activities and knowledge on how to live and survive there.

MATERIALS AND TOOLS

Tell me about the different materials for woodcut printing. Where do you source them?

Rizo: We purchase our plywood from Kota Kinabalu. We need to rent a van to travel to Kota Kinabalu. If it rains, there'll be

Large pieces of 8 x 4 feet prints are produced collectively with the village community.

Laying out the woodcut for printing in Labuan (2017). After inking the design, the whole community is invited to step on it, applying pressure evenly to imprint it onto cloth.

PANGROK SULAP

Woodcut print on paper. Expressing Pangrok Sulap's resolute solidarity with the villages. 'Behind me, there are villagers, Behind the villagers, there is me', meaning 'I have their backs, they have mine'.

PANGROK SULAP

sinkholes on the road and it'll take a long time.

Jerome: We use MDF[10] board now for woodcuts. We found a supplier in Kota Kinabalu. Previously, we used plywood but its wood grain does not allow for detailed carving. Lino is also very suitable but in Sabah, contrary to Semenanjung (Peninsular Malaysia), it is difficult to find and expensive to buy. Whereas MDF board is cheaper here and expensive in Semenanjung.

What about the inks?

Jerome: That was our other big challenge. I had to travel to Semenanjung to replenish our ink supply. One day, the supplier in Semenanjung asked where I was from. I replied, 'Sabah,' and he said, 'Why are you buying here? This is available in Sabah.' We did not know that that there was a supplier here in Kota Kinabalu.

Memet: Even then, it is still a two-hour long drive to buy the ink.

Jerome: Now we use offset ink. I believe most of the artists in Semenanjung also use offset ink.

Rizo: Maybe one day, we hope to use natural ink made from plants. We can teach villagers to produce their own ink and [do their own] printing.

Memet: Squid ink could be an alternative.

Jerome: That will be difficult. Squid ink is water-based. Oil-based black ink will always have a chemical component. I have seen soy oil-based ink, but it is not suitable for our boards. I have seen plant-based green and yellow ink, but not red. So we need to explore more.

You recently started producing your own papers?

Jerome: We are fortunate that Sabah has an abundance of banana trees.

Rizo: In fact the name 'Sabah' is from the banana – '*Pisang Saba*'.

Jerome: We are the largest banana producers in Malaysia.

Rizo: Jerome has a paper making workshop at home.

Jerome: The idea came when I was looking for ways to NOT buy paper. Also, the type of paper and size of paper that we need for our art is too expensive. I first made paper for myself and turned it into a book. People were taken aback when they realised it was handmade. Before long, I was getting orders from family members and friends!

I received a grant from the *Yayasan Inovasi*[11] to produce paper, which I will begin early next year (2018).

What about for large scale works?

Jerome: We use cloth. When you print on cloth rather than paper, the effect tends to be more faded. But using blackout cloth gives us the best result because it has a smooth texture and it's also more durable.

Rizo: For large-scale works, we need to attach multiple boards together. Our largest work is eight feet x twelve feet.

Jerome with samples of home-made paper made from banana stems.

WORKING PROCESS

Explain your working process and how you negotiate the different roles within the collective

Memet: Our roles in the group change annually. For example, this year I may take over managing the finances, but next year I may be in charge of customer service or pitching. The idea behind this is to see that each of us can take on multiple roles and the leadership of the collective is not left to one person. The responsibility is spread out to ensure that we guide each other and that each of us are capable of leadership.

Can you reflect upon working together as a loose collective? What are some of the challenges you face?

Bam: As a collective, we have to think about how to make decisions.

Memet: We all have our own ideas. So, we have learned that the best way to run the meeting and talk about our ideas, is to do it in a positive manner. Being positive makes problem solving easier.

Bam: Yeah, everyone needs to come and share their own experience [on the issue at hand], then only can we decide which solution is the best. Sometimes we have to combine the ideas… And if we face an impasse, we go back to the one who is in charge of the project.

Jerome: So it depends on who owns the project or who got the deal in the first place. That final decision goes back to that person.

How do you keep yourselves motivated?

Rizo: This collective is our family in addition to our own families.

Memet: Our little family

Bam: Our big family!

Jerome: Yeah, it's growing…

Rizo: Pangrok Sulap is a family. The collective emerged naturally as an offshoot. We just *became* a collective because we started 'doing things collectively'. What brings us together is the sense of belonging in a family. For example, when there's an event, we just ask our friends, 'Who wants to join us?' Whoever is free and available will join us. Then when we meet new people at an event, we eat together and work together. So when we leave, we all feel a sense of missing

Brainstorming session at their shop lot studio in Ranau (2017). Background, framed early prints produced in 2010 in the top row, followed by more recent work and merchandise.

Screen printing of 'Beads Not Dead', using a home-built screen-printing exposure unit for T-shirt printing.

After applying light sensitive photopolymer emulsion on the screen and letting it dry out, the image is printed onto a transparent sheet and placed between the light and the silkscreen. Rizo exposes the image to the spotlight between three to five minutes.

A high pressure water spray gun is used to wash out the emulsion.

After the wash-out process, a reverse stencilled image is revealed.

The process of printing patches based on the woodcut poster entitled 'Beads Not Dead'.

Rizo printing T-shirts for one of his customers.

the others. When we return to the same place, we are like long lost friends.

Bam: Yeah that's how it is for us. We can't wait to get together.

Rizo: It's about friendship. We put love first.

Jerome: We are always prepared to teach, and always prepared to learn. Even if I'm on a holiday, I don't mind giving a workshop. Because when we share what we know, automatically people will do the same.

What and who is involved in the design process?

Rizo: When we go to the villages we do a workshop and we teach skills only. This helps them to produce their own posters and fight for their own rights. We also research some of the issues they are facing, and then we brainstorm together and produce banners collectively.

Jerome: From the woodcut designs, we then produce T-shirts. Like for the 'Stop Kaiduan Dam' T-shirts, when we wear them, people will ask us, 'What is this about?' This gives us a chance to tell people that these are artworks produced by the *kampung* folk themselves. We just help them spread the word.

Bam: Also another advantage is that whatever we earn from the proceeds is returned to the people in the *kampung*.

How often do you meet as a group?

Memet: Usually, we find time to meet once a month. Whether we want to or not, we still do it. We take care of the studio together. That's how we stay together.

Jerome: But we don't force anyone, because we know everyone has their own responsibilities. Usually we fix it on a Thursday, but maintain some flexibility and play it by ear. As long as we meet once a month, it's good.

How many members do you have right now and how does one actually join the collective?

Rizo: About 10 to 15 of us. There's Rray, a full time tattoo artist who is in Sarawak right now. He joins us whenever he can. And there's Gindung, Wan, Ilya, Gery and others. Jib is our newest member.

Anyone can join us. Because to us, everyone is a teacher and a student at the same time. When someone new joins us, they always have something new to share with us. That's what we love about being in a collective. The more people you know, the more you will learn. So, if you're asking if there are any criteria for joining the group, no – there is none at all.

Saffwan and Bam, the print behind was produced in 2015 at Irregular Rhythm Asylum, Shinjuku, Tokyo, by Japanese art collective 'A3BC', (Anti-War, Anti-Nuclear and Arts of Block print Collective) for an exhibition titled 'From the foot of Mount Kinabalu to the foot of Mount Fuji.'

Jib: I joined Pangrok about a year ago. What I love about this collective is that you are always welcome, and you are treated like family. We are from difference races and religions but there is no discrimination here.

Notes

1. Mount Kinabalu is believed to be the spiritual abode of departed ancestors for the local Kadazan-Dusun natives, therefore it is revered for both its heritage and environmental values, beyond just a recreational spot.

2. Marjinal is an Indonesian punk rock group founded in Jakarta in 1997. This influential group was at the forefront of protesting social injustices with their music, and fanning the fires of social revolution that eventually brought about the fall of Suharto.

3. Taring Babi is an art collective led by Marjinal in 1997, Jakarta, Indonesia, focusing on activism through punk music and art.

4. Taring Padi is an Indonesian art collective established in 1998, Yogyakarta. Their works have been documented and critiqued in *Taring Padi: Seni Membongkar Tirani* (Paddy Tusks: Art Smashes Tyranny) (2011).

5. Pangrok Sulap's early protest posters included a series ('Menjual Salah, Membeli Salah', 'Sigup Nenek', 'Kirai Asli Original') that critiqued the local authorities for banning the sale of sigup, which has been a traditional trade and major source of income for the local communities of Sabah. Sigup refers to traditional hand-rolled cigarettes made from varieties of locally produced tobacco, usually sold with dried nipah palm leaves called *kirai* for rolling, or with gambier leaves for chewing.

6. The interview was done in 2017, but after that, Pangrok moved to a location in Kota Kinabalu in 2018.

7. 'ESCAPE from the SEA' was a collaborative art project, between The Japan Foundation Asia Center and the National Art Gallery (NAG) of Malaysia, that invited artists to explore the geopolitics of belonging to the Southeast Asian archipelago. Two of Pangrok Sulap's woodcut prints (one at the NAG and one at Art Printing Works in Bangsar), were taken down by the organisers, leading to an outcry on social media by the local art community over increasing art censorship.

8. The proposed Kaiduan Dam promises to increase water supply to Kota Kinabalu and its nearby districts, but at the cost of displacing hundreds of families living in the Ulu Papar area. Announced in 2009 by the Sabah state government, it is still pending review amidst resistance from the affected villages and protest from local and international NGOs.

9. Kampung Buayan, located within the deep jungles of the western Coast of Sabah, is one of the villages affected by the proposed Kaiduan Dam construction.

10. Medium-density fibreboard (MDF) is an engineered wooden product, made of wood fibre residue combined in a wax and resin binder, and formed into panels via the application of pressure and high temperatures.

11. Yayasan Inovasi Malaysia (YIM, the Malaysian Innovation Foundation) is a government agency under the Ministry of Energy, Technology Science, Climate Change & Environment.

SUPPORTERS

Christina Siaw • Siaw Hooi Chuan • Siaw Siew Lee

Shyan • Trevor Vale • Soh Chee Khoon

Akiko Sugiyama • Lingam.K • Agoes Salim

Azzaha Ibrahim • Cameron Kang • Jean-Claude Du Bois • Jerry Drawhorn
Kat Fatland • Kelly-Ann Baptist • Lee Khai • Rafizah Abdul Rahman • Siaw Mei Li
Vernon Adrian Emuang • Yeok Eu

Chan Hong Ngee • Chan Hooi Theng • Chan Seow Hong • Eddy Izuwan Musa
Eugene Foo • Gan Chin Lee • Loke Poh Lin • Lucia Abramovich • Mabel Dunn
Ong Hock Khoon • Ronnie Tan • RogueArt • Roshan Thiran • Sharaad Kuttan
T. K. Sabapathy • Tan Lai Kuan • Wang Cheng Yong

Choo Lub Hei • Christine Padoch • Clare Tan • Evelyn Teh • Fame Young
James Chong • Josiane Reggane • Kelvin Chuah • Kevin Chan • Larry Lam
Najua Ismail • Poh Swee Hiang • Shia Yih Phen • Sin Poh Poh
Wendy Teo Boon Ting • Wong Shou En • Zain Azahari • Azri Ahmad